Daddy, Can You Make Me Pancakes?

THE TRUE STORY OF A YOUNG MOTHER'S BATTLE
AGAINST CANCER AND HER HUSBAND'S JOURNEY
TO BRING HEALING TO THEIR FAMILY

Kevin McAteer

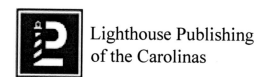

Lighthouse Publishing
of the Carolinas

PRAISE FOR *DADDY, CAN YOU MAKE ME PANCAKES?*

Kevin McAteer has created an important resource for anyone raising a family. Parents will treasure this book because it provides a rare, personal glimpse into one family's struggle with the loss of their mother — too young and too quickly. Kevin's candor and raw emotion will resonate with any reader dealing with cancer and the unfathomable need to explain loss to children. Kevin writes with honesty about a difficult situation and manages to find humor and lessons in everyday situations.

~**Amy Daniels**
Executive Director, Rex Healthcare Foundation

Daddy, Can You Make Me Pancakes? is not just a love story but an invaluable resource for any parent who needs to support a child dealing with a life-altering loss. Kevin's stories illustrate that grieving is an innate skill that's lost as we grow up and learn self-consciousness. Many adults don't know how to grieve, but this book shows that kids do. They cry, they get mad, then they go out to play.

~**Bonnie Rochman**
Former Staff Writer Raleigh News & Observer

There's so much to learn from this grieving husband and widowed father of three young children, yet you'll laugh through your tears. Kevin McAteer has the Irish knack for storytelling and a Pied Piper's charm, blended with down-to-earth humor, day-to-day spirituality, and an open heart. Daddy Will You Make Me Pancakes? honors his beautiful wife, only 36 years old when she died, with sweet and funny literary snapshots of their love for each other and their children. He also shares hard-won lessons for single fathers or mothers and anyone who's ever suffered loss.

~**Mary Bast,**
Ph.D., Psychologist and Author

Daddy, Will You Make Me Pancakes? is much more than a man sharing his story about the death of his wife and how he was thrust into being a single parent. This is a story that is witness to how the rawness of intense grief can be transformed into a powerful healing of the soul. It is story of affirmation that death does change relationship but that death does not end relationship. It is a testimony of the strength of the human spirit and the unending power of love. Daddy, Will You Make Me Pancakes? is a book of Hope and Healing.

~**Terri Kuczynski**
Patient Family Counselor, KidsCAN Coordinator, Rex Healthcare

Kevin McAteer's writes a sincere and heartwarming narrative about his family's journey through the loss of his three children's beloved mother and his loving wife. The story not only leaves a written family legacy, but also models a coping and self-treatment strategy: journaling the incredible memories that occur during a parent and husband's journey through bereavement of a spouse and interweaves his fortunate meeting of a lovely young woman who also has three children. His detailed description of their deep desire to create a loving home where their children have a complete family is so candid and real it will bring the reader to tears-both happy and sad. His honest, witty, sorrowful, hopeful, and sometimes humorous description of his family's life before, during, and after his wife's death can encourage other parents dealing with the death of a spouse to "keep on keeping on."

~**Dee Bostick**
Licensed Professional Counselor/ Registered Play Therapist

Kevin McAteer's deeply personal, heartfelt story will be a source of strength and encouragement for anyone who reads it.

~**Benny Williford**
President of Pinnacle Speakers Bureau

DADDY, CAN YOU MAKE ME PANCAKES? BY KEVIN MCATEER

Published by Lighthouse Publishing of the Carolinas

2333 Barton Oaks Dr., Raleigh, NC, 27614

ISBN 978-1941103180

Copyright © 2014 by Kevin McAteer

Cover design by writelydesigned.com

Interior design by Sherry Heinitz: www.sherryheinitz.com

Available in print from your local bookstore, online, or from the publisher at:
www.lighthousepublishingofthecarolinas.com

For more information on this book and the author visit: www.daddymakemepancakes.com

Brought to you by the creative team at LighthousePublishingoftheCarolinas.com:
Eddie Jones, Rowena Kuo, and Kevin Spencer.

Library of Congress Cataloging-in-Publication Data
McAteer, Kevin

Daddy, Can You Make Me Pancakes? / Kevin McAteer 1st ed.
Printed in the United States of America

Table of Contents

CHAPTER ONE

A Father's Note

"Smile through the tears."

December 8, 2011

Dear Kevin Patrick, Amanda, and Christopher;

The following is a collection of writings I captured during the somber days of Mommy's terminal illness and those that followed her passing on to heaven. These stories define my personal memories of the incredible love and marriage your mom and I shared and explain the extraordinary woman who will always be known by you as, "Mommy."

As the years go by, it will be harder for the four of us to remember the soft sound of her voice and gentleness of her touch. In the end, my hope is to have brought to life the many stories of our time together. Stories you possibly can't recall or were never caught on film for you to experience. Although I am sad she isn't here to watch you grow and equally sorry the time you had with her was short, I can promise you that all the good coming to you in this life will be because of her heart, soul, and spirit. I can also promise you there is a place called heaven. Why she had to go so soon, I do not know, but only in a place like heaven would they let such an angel spend eternity. Someday, a long, long time from now, when it's our turn to go to heaven, she will be there, just as we remember her, waiting to hug, kiss, and give you her warm, unconditional love.

The three of you have been my salvation. It's ironic how, during such a time of despair, it happened to be the three youngest people I know who saved and helped me carry on the job Mommy left me to finish—raising you. Your relatives may tell you how great a father I am, but you must know your Mom was the love that molded who you are today. She gave our family the foundation to be so excited to live each day to its fullest. I am so proud of each of you. You each have so many of her qualities that every day when I hug you, kiss you, and tell you I love you, it feels as though it's Pamela, your mom, that I am wrapping my arms around.

Kevin Patrick, so much of Mommy I see in you. You were her first child and lucky to have been raised by her the longest. It is Mommy's gift of emotion that she has passed on to you. She had an intense emotional energy about her, which made her love others so dearly. This high level of emotion is why you, like Mommy, can be the most kind-hearted person anyone could know. But that emotion can also explain why life hurts so much for you at times. Fortunately, like Mommy, when life hurts, you soon find the good in the world. You have Mommy's *heart*.

Amanda, you were Mommy's little buddy. She adored taking you everywhere she went, the 'two blondes skipping through life.' You are an amazing little girl. Like Mommy, so many will be amazed at your outer beauty and learn in a short period of time how you're even prettier on the inside. You may find out how having such innocent kindness can be taken advantage of at times, but don't let it change you. Like Mommy, you may never recognize this special beauty the rest of us can see, but know it is a gift. You have Mommy's inner beauty, her *soul*.

Christopher, Mommy treasured every minute she had with you. She loved you so much. She wanted you to be her two-year-old little baby boy forever. She often compared you to fun-loving cartoon characters, one being Curious George, the cartoon monkey. You were so cute, fun, playful, innocent, and always getting into things. You are blessed with Mommy's uncanny love of life. You have Mommy's *spirit*. Be aware though, it is that kind of free spirit that can get you into trouble at times, but it is what people will adore about you the most.

Smile through the tears, as Mommy would have.

With all my love and heart... *DADDY*

CHAPTER TWO

Pancakes—What Keeps Us Together

If it were not for my kids, I may not have gotten out of bed for a long time.

It's 6:15 a.m. on a Sunday morning. I'm asleep in my bed when a quiet voice sounds in my ear. The cute little blonde girl in the ponytails says, softly and innocently, "Daddy… can you make me some pancakes?" I respond with my eyes half shut and a slight smile on my face. "Sure honey, I'm coming right down." In that moment, Amanda and I escape the pain of the horror we shared just twelve short hours ago.

That Sunday morning was February 18, 2007, the morning after I had to find the words to tell Amanda (four years old), Kevin Patrick (six years old), and Christopher (two years old) their Mommy had died.

After the unexpected, painful loss of my wife, were it not for my kids, I would not have gotten out of bed or maybe the bottle for a long time. Literally and spiritually, Amanda did indeed get me out of that bed and that four-year-old voice reminded me of my "calling" to finish the job Pamela and I started, which was raising our three children in a warm and loving home.

In the real world I call it, "making pancakes."

A short minute later I was walking down the stairs with Amanda. I hit the ground running (okay, slowly shuffling) making her breakfast. Though the rest of that day is a blur, I'm sure it continued with two more little customers, more pancakes, and a lot of Daddy time to save the four of us from the reality of what cancer had painfully served us.

When I think back to that day and that time in my life, the continuing theme is, "Pancakes." Why?

Pamela's parents divorced when she was at a young age, causing her and her brother to live through the disputes of co-parental custody and visitation time. What I remember about my first meeting with her father, Art, was the pancakes. Pamela told me one of her favorite things—when he had her for visitation weekends—was his homemade pancakes. That memory carried all the way into her twenties, when I met Art for the first time at his beach house. All I can remember from that nervous first visit was Pamela telling me, "Wait until you eat my Dad's pan-cakes tomorrow morning. They're going to be the best you ever had."

Pancakes were a source of bonding for Pamela and her father during a time of uncertainty and sorrow. Pancakes were the only source, I think, that Amanda could come up with that early Sunday morning to soften her pain and confusion, and save me from crying in her arms again. These days that theme continues. My fiancée, Shayna, is divorced with co-custody of her children. At a time of feeling out-of-place and guilty, she too used her handed-down pancake recipe to bond with my kids.

So why pancakes? Pamela's dad probably cooked them one morning because it was the only thing he could whip up. Shayna had her recipe passed down through the family tree. And me? I used the microwave to heat up a box of pre-cooked frozen pancakes.

Maybe the pancake holds the secret of life's happiness. Life, like the pancake, doesn't have to be complicated. You can have others help you with them, you can pass the recipe on to the next generation and in a time of despair, pancakes may be the very thing that can bond neighbors, strangers and especially loved ones together. Most importantly, pancakes can put the biggest smile on a young child's face!

I believe the alarm clock makers of this world have missed out on a sure payoff, the best-sounding alarm a parent could ever hear in a time of despair, "Daddy… can you make me some pancakes?"

....

CHAPTER THREE

Dear Abby, The Other Night I Met This Girl and...

Real love takes a little longer than an after-work cocktail!

March 23, 1996
Dear Abby,

The other night I received a call from a close friend who was relocating at the end of the week to another part of the country. I was very close to Brad and his wife Tina, and they tried to convince me to join them for a farewell drink after work since I wouldn't get to see them again. I tried to brush them off, as it was the middle of a tiring work week and they were ready to live it up before heading off to a cruise the next day. I thought I had the upper hand until Tina explained she worked with a very attractive girlfriend and she and Brad wanted to introduce the two of us as their last achievement before leaving Philly.

Brad and Tina were right. Their friend was absolutely gorgeous, funny, and intriguing. To put it simply, this cool chick knocked me off my feet. I assumed she felt the same way since we stayed out until way after midnight, hours after Brad and Tina had left to rest up before their big trip. I thought I'd found the one. That was until I tried calling her a few days later, only to find she'd given me a non-working phone number. What do I do? How could I have been so wrong about her?

Sincerely,
Desperately Confused!

Dear Desperately Confused,

I know this probably hurts to hear, but sometimes that's how women these days innocently and, in some cases, safely break off a relationship. I'm sure she enjoyed meeting you. Otherwise, either her friend would have saved her before leaving, or she would never have stayed out later with you. A privilege we're blessed with as mature adults is the ability to decide who we spend our free time with, as well as the right to change our minds even if for no apparent reason. The tough love advice you need to hear is, "Just get over it and move on."

My advice to you moving forward would be to not let this moment prevent you from trusting those close to you when they think they have someone who might be compatible and interesting for you to meet. Next time, however, no matter how smitten you are at that first encounter, please give it more time before your inner cupid convinces you, "She's the one." Real love takes a little longer than an after-work cocktail!

August 30, 1997
Hey, Dear Abby,

It's me, Desperately Confused; I have two things to say. First, today she married me and that was the night my life changed forever. Second, you can bite me, because your advice column stinks.

Sincerely,
Happily Ever After!

Okay, I didn't actually write to an advice column. But a few days after meeting Pamela I was feeling pretty empty and lost. I think I was close to calling some kind of depression hot line after hearing over and over again the operator say, "*The number you have dialed is no longer in service; please hang up and try the number again.*" I was acting like a cat burglar, trying all different numerical combinations despite what was undeniably clear penmanship, and only one possible phone number, she'd written on that restaurant napkin.

As the weekend approached, I was certain I'd never hear from the mysterious, beautiful woman. She had unexpectedly walked into my life, stole my heart, and then quickly vanished. Pamela had told me she was going to Vermont that weekend with her Mom, and Tina and Brad were unreachable on their cruise out in the Atlantic. It was like a missing person's case. You know, where they tell you those first 48 hours are critical. Once it goes into the third day, the chances of ever seeing the person again drop dramatically.

That weekend was one of the most boring of the year. All I could do was try to distract myself from the truth and, when I couldn't, I would just stare into space, driving myself crazy with what could have been. Until Sunday afternoon…when I received an unexpected call on my cell phone. The caller I.D. popped up as a restricted number so no digits appeared. I was not in the mood to get a telemarketing call or talk to some distant friend or relative. Do I answer it? Do I let it go to voicemail? What if they don't leave a message? *OH MY GOD, WHAT IF IT'S HER AND SHE DOESN'T TRY TO CALL AGAIN? ANSWER THE PHONE, DUMMY. HURRY, ANSWER THE PHONE!*

I did. It was Pamela. I was pacing all over my apartment, acting like an eighth grader about to ask the most popular girl in school to the dance. Should I behave cool and confident, or let on about my confusion and curiosity? I decided to be honest, to tell her how happy I was she called and how distraught I'd been all weekend, thinking I might have totally misread the flirting and engaging conversation Tuesday night. I didn't reveal that I was also thinking about that memorable good night kiss.

Pamela was surprised. I thought she might not have been interested in me. She was clearly excited to talk to me and I had her immediately giggling with my rollercoaster tales of the past few days, and the mystery of the wrong number. She quickly had me floating on air again!

Pamela confirmed that I did have the correct phone number, but she had to make this call from a pay phone because…she stopped in midsentence…

The next thing I heard was a scream, what sounded like a muffled phone or a tussle between two people, then the stunning sound of a dial tone. She was gone.

Oh my God, what happened?

Did she have second thoughts?

Is there a jealous boyfriend I didn't know about who just caught her on the phone with me?

Had she been mugged?

Why did she have to call me from a pay phone? Was she running from something?

I willed my cell phone to ring.

How did this happen twice in seven days? This mysterious woman had played my heart again. I sat there staring at the phone. Two minutes went by, then five minutes. Nervously, I tried to call her confirmed home number only to be ticked off by the same recording I'd heard twenty times already. It was over. I decided I needed to walk away from this craziness. I left the phone on the kitchen table and grabbed my coat to go out for a while. As I closed the door, I heard my phone buzz. I JUMPED AT THAT PHONE.

It was Pamela. There was no jealous boyfriend, no mugger. Only a stranger on a bike riding along the sidewalk who didn't see her on the phone until it was too late and crashed into her. The good news? He got mostly the telephone pole, so she was in much better shape than 'Lance Armstrong' and his dinged-up bike. I also found out why the need for a pay phone. There were two reasons; both attributes I would learn to know and love about Pamela. First, she never paid her phone bill on time— not because she was broke—but because she lived care free, working very hard but not worrying about the small stuff like credit scores and making sure her utilities were in good working order. She, of course, had no idea it was past due until she couldn't dial from her apartment on Sunday after returning from Vermont. The second reason was that she couldn't wait to hear my voice and reconnect, so she found the first phone she could, which was a pay phone one block from her apartment.

We made sure we didn't leave love to chance. I got her address, read it back to her six times, then hopped in the car to head into the city where she lived, to pick up where we'd left off five days earlier.

That would be the last time Pamela would ever let go of my heart.

....

CHAPTER FOUR

There is No Book for That

"Is this how much it will hurt forever?"

Similar to a war veteran who carries memories of death in his mind and soul, some things are better left buried. Even as I type these words, I'm not sure it does any good to describe the night I had to let the children know their Mommy had left us, except I think it's an obvious curiosity they'll have as they grow older—trying to remember how they started to live without her. For that reason, I'll skim through the numbing moments as I left the hospital and made my way home, knowing I had to give the most difficult speech of any man's life.

As I left the ICU, a thin woman appeared out of the shadows and with a thick South African accent said, "Sir, let me help walk you out." Of all the hours and days I'd spent at the hospital, I'd never set eyes on this woman. It was as if I was no longer alive and she was an angel sent to guide me to meet with St. Peter. Unfortunately, the haze of white and gray surroundings she walked me through weren't the gates of heaven, only the drab hospital hallways or—as it seemed to me at that time— hell. I followed her to the left and to the right, for the first time completely unfamiliar with where I was in the hospital. I'm not sure I was even walking. In a coma of sorrow, no emotion on my face, no feeling in my bones, and no lift in my step, I glided down that haunted hallway like a ghost, carrying a pillow under one arm and Pamela's wedding rings in my hand. Both had been given to me by hospital personnel, as if they were paid tickets to this horrific ride. Finally, after a maze of turns, we started down a familiar hallway and I knew we were close to the hospital's lobby entrance.

I wanted to walk past her to avoid any conversation, but, as we came upon the final turn leading out of the hospital, the woman suddenly stopped. "Sir, is there anything else I can do for you right now?" Her face wore such a complex expression, one of pure kindness with a backdrop of sorrow, for the man who stood before her.

I knew my next step would start the walk to my kids. Turning to her, and wishing my words wouldn't bring her sadness. I replied, "Yeah. Do you have any advice as to how I'm supposed to explain to our three little children their mom is gone?" I knew it was an unfair question to ask, but it was the only thought I had at that moment. With surprisingly little hesitation the woman turned to me, a gentle smile on her face, and said in her thick accent, "Tell them their mommy is okay. She is in heaven with God now."

I looked down at the hospital floor, then up to her face, and then stuttered, "Okay. Thanks." And started off on my journey into a world that seemed so unfamiliar to me. A world Pamela was asked to leave behind.

I made it out of the hospital, trying to find some memory of where my car might be. It had been late morning with the sun burning bright when I'd received an urgent call from Pamela's mom and rushed to the hospital. Now it was night, as dark as a forest, and all I wanted was to hide inside our van. Somehow I stumbled upon where I'd parked. As I made my way to the car and reached for my keys to open the door, it dawned on me that I still carried Pamela's pillow under my arm. It had the fragrance of life on it, from the night she last lay on it, with a bare hint of perfume and the clean scent of shampoo from the woman I loved. At the same time, I noticed the sign of death, a stain at the end of the pillow case from a few drops of blood. Nonetheless, it held her scent and I had to take it with me. I got in, closed the door, and grabbed the steering wheel, realizing I had probably 15 minutes before I would pull into our driveway needing the exact words to explain to the kids.

I wanted to see my children so badly, as if seeing them was to cling to the life I had just left behind, yet wanted the drive to last much longer so I could have an easily memorized speech ready to deliver. I kept mentally repeating the words of the Nigerian-looking woman, adding my own heartfelt rhetoric. For the first time in eight months, every one of the 13 traffic lights between the hospital and our home was green. I knew there were 13 because in the preceding months I'd felt so frustrated driving back and forth, wanting to quickly get home or to Pamela's hospital room, when almost 90% of the lights would turn red seconds before I approached. I'd started counting them each day in a rage of self-pity.

As I approached our housing development I mumbled the rehearsed words I was about to speak, and then an uncomfortable thought: *Where am I going to give this speech?* I knew several neighbors were at the house watching the kids, waiting for me to arrive. I parked the van and started up our front sidewalk, leaving the pillow behind but carrying the rings tightly in my fist. I walked into our home with a smile like the woman had who escorted me from the hospital. Sincere, but reflecting little joy. I saw stacks of pizza boxes on the kitchen table and heard the normally fulfilling chants of, "Daddy, Daddy's home." I remember my friend, Chris, was standing next to my sons and we locked mutually bloodshot eyes, both nodding. As a father himself, I could sense him feeling the pain and sadness of what I was about to do.

I said "Hi" to our neighbor Ms. Pong and Chris's wife Julie, then asked the kids to come upstairs to visit with me for a few minutes. They followed me up the stairs and into my bedroom, thrilled that one of their parents had arrived home and asking with joy in their voices how Mommy was, completely unaware their lives were about to change forever.

There isn't a book with instructions for a father who has to deliver such news. Even though I'd gone over it a hundred times in the van minutes earlier, I had no idea what to say. If there were a guide, I'm pretty sure it wouldn't cover how to give such a speech in as few words as possible while making sure not only your six-year-old hears you, but your four-year-old understands, and the two-year-old has at least some comprehension.

I wanted to break the news as quickly and as simply as I could. A few steps into my room, I got down on the floor on my knees. Kevin Patrick eagerly sat on the floor next to me leaning on my shoulder, Amanda rested in my lap as if we were going to read a bedtime story. Energetic Christopher stood on my leg, barely reaching my eye level. I looked deeply into their eyes and their faces quickly turned from joy to worry as I slowly delivered the words. "Guys, Mommy has died. She died today and has gone to heaven. Her spirit is with us but I'm so sorry, we will never get to see her again."

I'll never forget that moment, although I've tried for more than six years. I know Kevin Patrick fully comprehended the finality of the situation. When I told him Mommy had gone to heaven, he knew what the news meant intellectually, understanding about cancer, as well as emotionally, feeling the pain of losing his mom. I think Amanda understood that these words brought pain, but I often wonder—as she lay in her bed that night—if she was sure it would be forever. I could sense that Christopher, nearly two years old, was confused and saddened by Kevin and Amanda crying out in pain. We quickly embraced, our arms tightly wrapped around a family of four, wishing there were two more arms surrounding us.

Just replaying those moments brings such painful flashbacks. As blurry as my memory grows, trying to remember all the great moments of our lives together, what remains vivid is what happened in that Intensive Care Unit, the walk out of that hospital, and the moment I expressed such loss to our children.

I describe those events in detail to convey how deeply our lives changed that day. Grieving took on many cycles for me in that I lost my wife, my closest and dearest friend, lost being the father I once was, and was forever a different friend and family member. Those first few days were god-awful, then the grief lessened as I was overwhelmed with decisions and the constant supervision and concern for the children. Then it had its peaks and valleys for weeks and weeks as I often walked around numb. The real world of continuing to raise the kids butted up against the career that was on hold, but both were now demanding my attention. Months went by as I tried to settle into some kind of normalcy, experiencing okay days, and then really painful, low days wondering,

"Is this how much it will hurt forever?"

The most painful loss to endure, and the one that hurts the most, still, is that Kevin, Amanda and Christopher were short changed, and so was Pamela as a mother. They had the greatest mom any kid could dream of, and they were any mom's dream come true as well-mannered, loving babies.

No. There was no text book to guide me through the night of Feb 17th. No lesson to be taught, no book to read, but at least I now know there is one chapter in a book somewhere of how one dad and three little children made it through.

....

CHAPTER FIVE

The Wedding Cake

What I wouldn't do to walk just one more mile with mono
in my system and one black shoe on my foot.

August 30, 1997. The day Pamela and I were married. That day and the weekend that followed summarized so well the couple we became, the personalities we were known for, and the life we would be blessed with for many years to come.

We had a great day from beginning to end. The sun was shining but we were spared the typical summer humidity. There was no in-law bickering, no bridesmaid falling down on her job, no groomsman throwing up from the night before. The ceremony went without a hitch. We moved from the church to an outdoor cocktail reception on the lawn of the old-fashioned fire station where we hosted our wedding reception, better described as a wedding *party*! Pamela had looked forward to this day her whole life. It was awesome to see her eyes sparkling and her smile gleaming the entire day, and not just when the pesky photographer would say, "Okay, just one more shot." She looked stunning in her wedding dress, and no one would have believed this professional fashion retailer was wearing a gown that cost less than $200.00. She was my dream girl, but the way she looked that day she could have been every man's dream girl.

The party that followed was a night of laughs, strange situations, and a couple of 'oops' but we never let any of it affect how special and perfect the day was turning out to be. You'd think many might talk about our first dance together, or my brother's heartfelt toast, but I had a feeling several other moments resonated in the hundred or so guests who joined us on our first day of marriage.

The reception on the lawn was a perfect combination of weather, food, cocktails, storytelling, and music. The only strange note actually, was the music. Not that it wasn't a perfect song list, but when you looked over at the portable keyboard piano you'd hear music, see the keys moving up and down, but no piano man could be found. "Wait! There he is having a cocktail at the bar and talking to your Uncle Pat." Pamela cracked up, asking me, "Didn't we pay him to play the music or is he just here to make sure we *have* music?"

Members of the band that night were much better musicians, luring everyone off their chairs and into the celebration. The only "whoops" was that I don't think they knew they'd be playing in an old firehouse. We thought the manager who visited the firehouse with us during our planning stages would have figured out we'd need additional lighting when the sun went down. We ended up dancing in what felt like a bedroom with a nightlight on. In a way, this added to the "Let's just celebrate" mood.

My favorite moment, of course, was the traditional "Groom Pulls Garter Belt Out From Under New Bride's Gown." Normally I find traditional wedding reception stuff corny, but I had a game plan in place weeks prior to our wedding, to make sure I made a statement during this normally goofy tradition. Members of my family, being from Philadelphia, were avid Philly sports fans. Pamela's family is from New Jersey and they're as fanatical about their New York/New Jersey sports teams. Typically it would be highly recommended the two families never meet and especially don't marry. It's a recipe for disaster and confrontation. However, on this day everyone put their brass knuckles and name calling aside to enjoy the union of two people and two great families. Until, of course, it came to garter belt time. Unbeknownst to Pamela and everyone else in the firehouse, I had a trick up my sleeve. Literally up my sleeve. As I reached under Pamela's dazzling white gown, I slowly un-tucked from my left sleeve a three foot long Philadelphia Eagles football pennant. Moments later, to the shock of Pamela and the roar of half the crowd, I whisked my hands out from under my bride's dress, not to toss a garter belt but to unravel a sign of solidarity with my Philadelphia family and friends. The crowd cheered as I showed off my Green and White pennant, and Pamela sat there stunned, wondering how the hell I hid that under her dress without her knowing about it. I guess the champagne and lack of food were starting to catch up with her.

That would have gone down as the surprise of the night had it not been for my cousin Joe, nicknamed Mug Man, because of the frequency he had a beer mug in his hands at football games. Late in the night Joe surprised us by asking Pamela's 90-year-old grandmother to dance with him. We were even more surprised that she said yes.

The party had ended and we were dropped off at a local hotel to consummate our marriage. We were worn out from the day's events but nonetheless extremely happy. Our night didn't end as it does sometimes in stories, no gazing into one another's eyes, sharing a kiss under the moonlight. No, it was pizza, sweatpants, and eerie TV time. That was the Saturday night every prime time channel stopped its normal broadcast to update the world on an unbelievable tragedy. Princess Diana had died in a car crash. On the first night of our life together we could not tear our weary eyes from news of the hard-to-believe loss of that good-hearted soul who was supposed to live well into her nineties. It just stuns me that both Princess Diana and Pamela were 36 years young when they passed away. Although that was a sad moment in history, it in no way dampened our special day but sure made it one I'll never forget. If I was ever unsure of our anniversary date, I knew with a quick Google search about Lady Diana's death I could be certain I had the right day.

The next morning seemed to begin what some people say is the curse of marriage. There's a tale you only hear in men's locker rooms or at the local watering hole. It is about how the happiness men share in a relationship can go unfortunately sour with the taste of a unique food, the wedding cake. The wedding cake is said to immediately transform the woman the groom believed he was marrying, from an idolizing adoring spouse into a dictating princess. All of which can be linked to that first smash of icing in the face.

None of that was true in our case, but some very strange things happened the next morning when we awoke as a married couple. Many have heard of Cinderella and the glass slipper, but this morning it was the case of the missing black shoe. As you will learn, Pamela was fond of shoes. I cursed them, as she had tons of pairs of black shoes in closets throughout our home. That morning, I was able to lay claim to all the garments I'd rented from the tuxedo store with one exception. I was missing a black shoe. Our hotel was very nice and considered the place to stay in Summit, New Jersey; however it had to be one of the smallest rooms in the entire Northeast. How the hell did I lose a shoe in such a small hotel room? The hotel was close to Lyn's house (Pamela's mom). That's where we were to spend the day, having brunch with the immediate family and watching the Philadelphia Eagles and New York Giants play in the season's first football game. Pamela and I were a bit hung over, and it was such a nice day out we decided a walk in the brisk air would be healthy for both of us. So, off we went on our ten-block "Walk of Shame" to Pamela's mother's house, I with only one black shoe on.

The day didn't get any better for me as my father, brother and I watched the football game with five new in-laws in the basement of Lyn and Gus' house. Gus, Pamela's stepfather, a huge NY Giants fan, was itching to return the verbal abuse from the night before when I'd taunted them all with the Philadelphia pennant at the wedding reception. As you can guess, our team lost and we had to take the beating from our newly blended family.

The next morning I finally escaped the razzing of my in-laws. Pamela and I were off to our honeymoon. You would have thought our luck would improve as we flew out to Kauai for a week of fun and sun as newlyweds, but instead I came down with some type of bug that just whipped my butt. Each day, I would wake up in the late morning and go out for breakfast with Pamela, ready to talk about the awesome day ahead. Unfortunately, I would instead end up feeling ill after breakfast and have to go right back to bed. Then I'd get up around lunch time totally motivated to make up for the time lost, only to find myself physically drained and having to take another nap. This went on the entire week. When we got home Pamela insisted I go right to the emergency room while she unpacked the car from our wedding weekend and honeymoon. Although I felt terrible allowing my new wife to unpack the car alone, it wasn't any worse than how I'd felt napping on her the entire honeymoon week. Boy, she had to wonder what was in that wedding cake!

I went straight to the doctor. When he came back from looking at my blood work he said, "Well, you have mono. Do you know anything about mononucleosis?"

"Some type of kissing disease that gives you swollen glands?" I hopefully replied. The doctor ignored my sarcasm.

"I can tell you when someone is diagnosed with mono, we recommend a few very important things."

1. Don't travel
2. Don't drink much alcohol
3. Don't cut short a full night's rest.

Guess it was too late to follow doctor's orders.

All I could think is Pamela must be back at the house calling her friends and family, and thinking the "wedding cake curse" had resulted in the demise of the man she fell in love with. First, the big romantic wedding night bliss devolved into pizza on the bed and watching TV. Then a honeymoon week of naps, and now I have my bride unpacking the car by herself!

That wedding/honeymoon week really did sum up our marriage but not in the way you might think:

- We never took life too seriously but life always seemed to get serious on us, and at the most unfortunate times.
- We were always there for each other when the other was feeling down and out, or sick and tired. We never judged or second guessed the reasons why the other person was feeling off. We always knew we weren't the cause; it was just the way life played out that day.
- When one of us was ready to make fun of the other's family, meaning me of course, those damn New York Giants would pull off a big win!

On our first day of marriage I lost a shoe. Unfortunately nine years later, on the last day of our marriage, I had numerous pairs of women's shoes I had to slowly do away with. What I wouldn't do to walk just one more mile with mono in my system and one black shoe on my foot.

....

CHAPTER SIX

The Toughest Kid on the Block is Not Always the Meanest Looking

"Let's start tonight!"

Over the years I've seen many tough people, and I've come face to face with a few. I could also tell endless stories of the heroic moments in sports I've witnessed, but none would rival the grit I saw first-hand in April of 2006.

Prior to 2006, Pamela would not have made the list of top 100 toughest people, even if there were only 101 people in the world. Not because she was wimpy or a whiner. Toughness just wasn't what defined her. She led every day with her heart, with a childlike caring for all that was good in the world—not the type of person who normally makes the list of biggest bad asses on the block, though she didn't always have it easy growing up, and dealt with some tough stuff that most teenagers never have to experience. I learned back then and in 2006 that she wasn't like all the stereotypical people we would have naturally ranked ahead of her on the list. She was tough as nails when she had to be. But mean? No way. When she had to muscle up, she could do it from somewhere deep in her soul. That's because her heart by far was her strongest muscle.

The day we learned Pamela had leukemia, her world and ours shattered. Within hours of her being diagnosed, Pamela found out what having this type of cancer meant. She and I both heard from the doctors that it was going to take a lot more than a few needles in her arm or drawing blood from time to time to get her better. No, this was going to be more dangerous and painful for her, more than most people would experience during a lifetime. I could list the many tough procedures she had to endure, but that's not what I want to remember about those last ten months we spent with Pamela. In the face of this dangerous disease, Pamela was tough, but in her way—in a way I doubt I'll witness again.

In my years of playing high school and college football I heard many speeches from coaches, in the locker room or on the football field. Often they quoted great leaders who led men and women into deadly battles. There's one quote I've never forgotten from those years of playing football: "*A man who has courage is the one who has fear in his heart to do what is asked of him, but he goes anyway.*" If that's true, then Pamela was one of the bravest women I'll ever meet. The night we learned about her cancer, Dr. Crane gave her a choice, knowing how heart wrenching it was for her to not be home with the three kids. She could opt to go home for a few days to get mentally prepared for beginning chemotherapy. Or, if she thought she was ready, they could start the next morning on working to beat the cancer. She paused for an instant, glanced at me, then looked at Dr. Crane and said, "Let's start tonight!"

Pamela certainly was not the meanest looking chick in the neighborhood. She was the kind of pretty that no matter where she went she turned a few heads. Even when she rolled out of bed she looked beautiful and happy, as if she'd taken hours to put herself together. But that's not what separated her from those rough and tough dudes you might see on a football field or in a boxing ring. When it came to this heavyweight fight against cancer, she took the fight game to a new level.

After the first few days in the sterile environment of the hospital, Pamela was able to go home. Unfortunately she'd have to return to the hospital for three to six days every couple weeks to take on the chemo and her cancer. The second time she was more prepared. When we pulled up to the hospital I first had to park by the front lobby doors. Not because Pamela felt too weak to walk from the parking lot to the lobby. Oh no. I had to park there to unload bags and bags of decorative linens and other items for her room. Each time Pamela would arrive at the hospital she'd lead us down the hallway. She was like a champ walking down the long aisle of an arena, set to step through the ropes in front of thousands of screaming fans to take part in the battle of a lifetime. What separated this bad-ass woman from a boxing champ was that she brought the following with her when she stepped into the ring:

- Pink and purple bedspread
- Floral curtains to hang over the dull, white blinds
- A polka-dot trash can
- Matching pink shag carpet for her bathroom
- Vases of imitation flowers (real ones not allowed in a sterile environment)
- Paintings and pictures to hang on the walls that screamed, "This is a girl's room; beware, you mean cancer cells!"
- And, of course, bright pink and yellow pillows

I'm sure you think I'm exaggerating. You could only believe it if you saw it yourself. I remember two occasions when my hard work of dragging those bags of knick knacks and decorations for her room really paid off. The first time was a Tuesday morning when Dr. Crane entered Pam's room during her second visit to give an update on her diagnoses. I don't think I've ever seen anyone more stunned. Doctors are always ready to deal with the unexpected, but the smile on his face said he didn't expect the many pastel colors that nearly blinded him. He must have struggled to wipe it off his face when he left to see his next patient.

The second experience was truly the funniest thing I'll ever witness in a hospital, where there are so few enjoyable moments. Late one night, the hospital kitchen called Pamela's room to let her know it was her last chance to order dinner. From all the medicine they were shooting through her veins to kill the cancer cells, she had trouble finding the strength to eat. But she knew she had to eat, so she placed an order in hopes she might get some food down later in the night. After about thirty minutes, a hospital employee knocked on the door, announcing that his name was William and he had her dinner. As he entered the room with Pamela's tray I was taken aback, wondering, *Is this guy really a hospital employee?* When I tell you he looked like the toughest kid on the block, I'm not kidding. William was a tall, African American young man, his hair pulled back in dreadlocks, and strutting like a rapper. He didn't look very happy, I'm guessing because at that hour of the night he was probably ending a long work shift. As a matter of fact, he looked a bit cranky and intimidating.

But when he stepped all the way in and saw how Pamela had transformed this hospital room into something you'd find on a Home Makeover show, he couldn't control himself: "Damn! Holy cow, I've never seen anything like this before in this hospital. This room is amazing. Ms. McAteer, you should decorate all our rooms. This is unbelievable!"

I still crack up that a tough-looking young man was so blown away by floral curtains and pink shag carpet and a purple bedspread. I thought to myself, after I stopped laughing inside (because I was still a little intimidated by the looks of this guy I didn't want to openly snicker), *only Pamela could shed prejudice, cancer, and everything else there is to hate about hospitals and bring nothing but love out of a perfect stranger.* I wished I knew William's work schedule, just so we could order dinner every couple weeks and enjoy his reaction to the latest interior design trends. Not only did Pamela bring her room to life each time she entered it, but each time she bought a new set of color schemes and flashy décor pieces to keep the fighting ring full of energy. I wonder if she did it for herself or for those of us in her corner during the toughest, heavyweight rounds?

A few days after we found out she was no longer in remission Art had called her to console her. I overheard her on the phone reassuring her dad. "Daddy, I just want you to know I'm no longer depressed. Don't worry about me or be upset, thinking I'm sad. I have my boxing gloves on and I'm ready to go back in."

Little did she know we all viewed her as a world champion. She was a fighter with courage but also with flair. I doubt that any hospital will ever again see someone like Pamela, preparing herself in that sterile hospital room, ready to throw pink and purple punches at cancer.

CHAPTER SEVEN

Some Things a Widower Shouldn't Have to Decide

How in the hell do I make that decision and
more importantly, why do I have to make it?

As all of us grow older, we're encouraged not only to have our Will in place, but also to make arrangements that carry out our final wishes and ease the burden on our loved ones in mourning. Well, it would have been nice to have that advice in my mid-thirties.

I've never backed away from making important decisions. Not that I've made all the right choices, but I haven't cowered from the responsibility. Only days after losing Pamela and having to console three young kids, I had to write Pamela's obituary. I also had to make plans for her funeral, pick out her casket, make a decision on either flowers or donations for those who wanted to honor her, and other responsibilities I've probably blocked out.

When it came to the moment when I had to tell the cemetery caretaker where in the acres of grass I wanted my wife to be buried, I'd had enough. I wanted to say, "Why don't *you* figure it out? How in the hell do I make that decision and more importantly, why do I have to make it?"

Instead, I tried to reply respectfully. "Robert, I'm sorry. I have no idea how to choose a plot of grass and frankly, I just don't give a damn. You're a nice man and you've been very helpful so I trust you to make the decision."

Of course there was no way he was going to do that. I'm sure he'd lived with a lifetime of family members bitching at him for choosing the wrong section. Being the understanding professional he was, he said, "I can't imagine how difficult this is for you and the kids. I'll give you a few options that might make it easier for you to choose."

Well, guess what? I learned how to choose. Robert taught me how to decide whether it should be on a hill or a flat area of grass over acres and acres of land. I never wanted that knowledge, but I realized I needed it then and I'm glad Robert made me take the responsibility. In case you find yourself needing this kind of knowledge, the following points are what I was told to consider:

1. You don't want to be too far from the road if you have small kids, so when you visit they won't have far to walk.
2. Being close to the road when they're younger will also help them gain a better sense of the location, in the event they come as teenagers on their own.
3. You don't want to be too close to the cement through-way between cemetery sections, because visitors will accidently drive along the edge of the grass.
4. An open space where there aren't many burials will keep the setting private for a while, as your young children get used to what to do when they visit. There will be neighbors at some point, but for now it will feel a bit like their own place.
5. Pick a spot that has only one tree, so as soon as you drive to that section they'll see a basic landmark for her memorial.
6. The last suggestion, one I'd like to forget, is to pick a spot where you can reserve a place next to her in the unfortunate case that you pass early. You don't want your children to have to search over miles of field to find both their mom and dad.

All points are logical, all important to consider and, frankly, all are necessary.

Although Pamela hasn't yet had many people move in to her section in the cemetery, there was an emotional and memorable moment when we met the neighbors already buried there. It happened after Robert helped Lyn and me make our decision. I wandered aimlessly for a while amongst the scattered stone carved name plates that were spread out around the area we'd chosen for Pamela. The first stone we noticed belonged to a four-year-old child and the next, to a ten-year-old boy. The third stone belonged to a baby who had never made it to her first birthday. And, almost unbelievably, the fourth grave belonged to a young teenager born on the same date as Kevin Patrick.

Inadvertently, it appeared, in a cemetery with thousands and thousands of grave sites, we had chosen a resting place for Pamela that centered her among those she had most liked to be surrounded by in life, children. I want to believe somehow Pamela was up there gently pushing us to this location, so her memory on earth would continue to be surrounded by kids.

Then, for a moment, I was worried my kids would be scared when they read the dates on the stones. Would they fear they might die soon, as well? You know, sometimes you have to leave things in the hands of the Lord. I did, and it was the right thing to not over-think a beautiful honor we'd bestowed on Pamela.

I do have to comment on one other stone, the closest one to Pamela and the nearest one to our landmark tree. We know her as "Ms. Otto," not because that's engraved on her stone (although her last name is Otto), but because she was eighty years old when she was laid to rest. It appears there are only a few times in a year when Ms. Otto's family visits her. I smile when the kids either say "Hi" to Ms. Otto or we look for something fresh to leave in her vase, because we know that would be Pamela's desire as well. If she had to be near an adult, she would love it to be a grandmother she could hold hands with, smile, and laugh about the pure things in life—like being surrounded by innocent, loving children.

....

CHAPTER EIGHT

"Daddy, It's Going to be Okay."

Your boy knows you should be hurting. Be real with him, just let the tears go.

I was trying to get through each hour and figure out how to get the four of us through the rest of our lives without Pamela. My parents were staying with me for the week to help out and, of course, to be there for all of us emotionally. One day my mom was in the kitchen making lunch for all the kids and my dad must have been entertaining them prior to the lunch bell ringing. I stepped outside to sit on our front steps. Such a rare moment to breathe usually triggered grief, even when I didn't want to weep. As I sat with my head in my hands and a puddle of tears between my feet, I heard the storm door unexpectedly open behind me. It was Kevin Patrick. I knew I couldn't pull it all together quickly enough to hide my sadness, when an inner voice whispered:

Ah, just let it go,
Dad, just let the tears go.
Your boy knows you're sad;
Your boy knows you should be hurting.
Be real with him.

Kevin sat down next to me as I picked my head up and stared aimlessly at the front yard with the path of streaming tears still on my face and eyes full of more to follow. He put his arm around my shoulders and said:

"Daddy, I'm sorry you're sad. I miss Mommy, too, but it's going to be okay. I love you."
That might have been one of my proudest moments as a father.

Ask your friends how many of them have seen their mom or grandmother cry. You may be surprised to hear that very few have seen their role model for affection drop one tear. I'm here to tell you it is okay to cry in front of your kids, especially when a family is suffering from a great loss. I come from a very outwardly emotional family. The Irish can be that way. Still today, I hug my father, uncles, and my brother every time I see them. I can only recall seeing my Dad cry twice, before we lost Pamela, once at my grandmother's funeral, and once when I was very young and he was in some physical pain. But those two times were enough to know that crying in front of your children is healthy.

I like to believe Kevin Patrick learned a lot more by flipping roles that afternoon and being the one consoling me than he would living with the perception that fathers shouldn't show pain, and grandfathers should hide true emotions from the ones they love.

Don't let me misguide you. I shuffled away from my kids many days to unload a bucket full of sorrow, I abruptly shut my office door at work almost weekly to sob over reports on my desk, and I definitely turned my head and wept as I stared out the passenger window of many airplanes. We all need moments to ourselves, even if we can't be completely by ourselves.

However, if you want your children to embrace one great lesson and start a new tradition to hand down to the next generation, let them see it is okay for parents to cry, especially in front of their kids.

CHAPTER NINE

The One Time the S.P.C.A. Got My Attention

KidsCan! didn't cure her cancer, but it saved our family.

When you lose a loved one, it can be rough to wake up the next day to the business of death. It was especially difficult being the surviving spouse of a young married couple. There was no one else to turn to when I had to make dozens of decisions about Pamela's burial and service because every step of the way, I knew it was critical to consider the three little kids she left behind. As their father, it was my responsibility to make sure they weren't completely stunned by our loss, and allow them to find answers and establish memories in the reality we all faced. At the same time, I had to be sure not to put them in harm's way emotionally, without someone there to catch them when their hearts got broken. I was fortunate to have many people around me to take on much of the burden, but there still were tons of decisions only the husband/father could and had to make.

If you've never been through such a difficult process, consider yourself blessed. Not only are your emotions raw, but there's a stop watch on you to make these decisions within days. I can recall, after each step of the funeral process, I would disappear away from Pamela's parents and brother to privately unload all the emotion that had collected within me during those short periods of time. Responsibly, then, I would pull myself together and head back inside for the next round of decision making.

I respected how the funeral home and cemetery professionals tended to our needs, so I tried to be patient with the tasks they required. After the mental and emotional torture finally ended of completing the checklist at the cemetery, we were again herded off to the funeral home. I felt bad, knowing I'd been short-tempered choosing a gravesite, and wanted to be better prepared for what was coming next. In the car, I read a questionnaire we'd needed to work through at their office. The ride gave me just enough time to plan what decisions I could bear making, and which ones I'd refuse to deal with and politely delegate to someone else in the family or the funeral director. I had a quick mental response to one question in particular:

> #7. Please list the names of any charities you would like to request donations be forwarded to in the deceased's name in lieu of flowers, or specify if the funeral home should encourage friends and family to send flowers in the loved one's memory.

The first charity I thought of, obviously, was the American Cancer Society— which I hope you can understand was not my favorite nonprofit organization. In my grieving and ignorant state, I selfishly thought, *Why the hell do I want people to donate to the American Cancer Society? Millions have been doing that for years and what did it get us? Nothing, not a damn thing. All that work and money and Pamela will never see her children again. Screw that, screw them.*

I decided to encourage the offering of flowers. Not because I was mad at the world or against finding a cure for cancer, but if there was one person who would appreciate fresh flowers, it was Pamela. We'd lived with newly-cut fresh flowers in every room of our house because of her passion for their beauty. In theory, I do agree that all the money on flowers for a funeral is a waste, because they wither away and are gone weeks later. In Pamela's case, however, flowers would be as appropriate a sendoff as a 21-gun salute for a fallen soldier.

As we arrived at the funeral home and walked to the entrance, I split off from the group, telling them I'd be right in. I then went through my routine of grief, walking around the corner and weeping over the surreal reality that I was a widower before the age of forty. Then I wiped my eyes and headed back in for the job at hand.

We sat around a table, working through the list. As the funeral director moved to each new question, everyone would look at me as if I were the Pope or President, waiting to see if I would answer. I'd either give a short "Yes" or "No," or would say to Lyn, "You make this decision." Other times I would tell the funeral director, "Do what's most commonly decided." A few times, my plan of patient delegation or quick one-word answers were tested by the family, wanting approval for matters I just didn't care about. As an example, when the funeral director asked what music they would play during a certain section of the service, I said, "Lyn, this one is yours. You'll make the right decision." She would, and did, but then would ask, "Kevin, are you okay with that, or did you have other ideas?" I would keep it cool and plead, "Really, Lyn, some things I just don't care to decide, and I know you'll make the right choice."

I knew we were quickly heading to the charity or flowers part of the interview. I was prepared, but my intuition told me no matter what I said or how I presented it, I was going to hear a rebuttal from the table. So when the funeral director asked, I replied, "Normally, I'd think an overabundance of flowers is a bit of a wasted gesture," then offered a few reasons why it was different in Pamela's case. Also, in an effort to cut the expected response off at the pass, I was honest, saying I wasn't a big fan of charitable donations at this stage of our loss. Well, even at a time of extreme mental stress, my brain was right about reading the group around me. They presented a soft sell of why I might think we missed out on something special if we didn't encourage donations to a charity in Pamela's name.

I tuned everyone out as they spoke, almost as if I'd put plugs in my ears. I could see their lips moving but I could not hear the words. All I heard was, "Blah, blah, blah," while screaming internally, "Everyone just shut the hell up!"

Then, with extreme clarity, I heard "S. P. C. A." I stopped the white noise in the room and made the assistant funeral director repeat what she'd just mentioned. "You don't have to consider donations to such large, well-known organizations. You can use this loss to assist any organizations Pamela might have had a strong interest in."

My first reaction was, "Really? The S.P.C.A? That's what one would consider a charity?" The concept was interesting enough that finally someone in the room had caught my attention. Suddenly I gained back the strength of both my left and right brain. The other word I heard for the first time was, "Pamela." I asked for a few minutes to think about this decision. As everyone kept talking, I was thankful my head's selective sound blocking system was still functioning, so I could concentrate.

I liked the concept of something out of the box like the S.P.C.A.. It would have been at the top of Pamela's list. However, it's not on my "bucket list" of places to visit before my time here is through.

Then I dug deep into my noggin and finally dusted off a treasure chest with the perfect idea inside. I spit out the words, "KidsCan!" This caught Lyn's interest and also took her and everyone else by surprise. I jumped up on my soap box.

"Kids…children were Pamela's greatest love and passion. Our kids, your kids, any kids—that's what she'd want; for everyone to give money to the one program that did everything possible and still helps Kevin Patrick, Amanda, and Christopher through the effects of this dreadful disease. KidsCan! is the sole reason the five of us stayed a close, loving family through cancer. Although KidsCan! didn't cure her cancer, the people there saved us as a family. Pamela is gone, but KidsCan! is keeping me and our three kids together through this tragic time."

Little did I know, on one of my darkest days, at that table in the funeral home I would pull through an idea that would raise over $30,000 in the loving memory of the best mom you could ever have. That $30,000 ended up being the monetary answer to a vision of an educational DVD about the program to help thousands of families dealing with cancer. If the money donated helped just one small child, one time, emotionally stay the course of helping their parent beat cancer, then Pamela's passing from leukemia would not be for nothing, and our loss could be eased by the gain of a child in need. And all of this was possible because of the giving in Pamela's memory.

CHAPTER TEN

I Guess Stealing and Trespassing are Not Against the Law

*Sweating in fear, I would tear down flowers from those trees,
leaving limbs and a poor example for my kids behind.*

At some point upon our return from the funeral home, I had a brief moment of peace and found myself daydreaming while I aimlessly paced the backyard. The struggles earlier that day from having to make unfair decisions brought a flashback of challenging times Pamela and I would have welcomed back into this life's current reality.

My mind got lost into the year we became proud parents of our third child. Those days were quite a struggle each time I came home from work. Three kids, all under the age of four. Four! Sometimes our only saving grace was strapping the three of them in a stroller, hoping all of them or at least two of them or, damn, just one of them would fall asleep on the walk. Every night was the same routine, Kevin Patrick constantly chanting, "Da-Da-Dah-Daddy," Amanda bouncing her head back and forth pointing and yelling at every leaf, squirrel, and dog in sight, and Christopher—even at that early age—trying to grab Amanda's hair/hand/foot/ shirt, or anything else he could pull to torment her. Sleep was a rare happening. That's why, when we went for our walks, Mommy was in charge of juice boxes, bottles, and crackers, and Daddy was in charge of caffeine.

Their crazy ways weren't the only reason our walks would drive me nuts. It was because I also had to live through the stress of Pamela's trespassing, stealing, and defacing homes throughout the neighborhood. You see, at any given minute a flower would catch her eye out of nowhere that some home owner had planted and grown to make both their home and the neighborhood look pretty. Pamela had a weakness. If she saw a flower she liked, and that happened often, she would just walk, no…wait, rather she'd sneak up to the plant, or tree and SNAP, take one or two of those flowers right out of the homeowner's yard. Depending on where you've lived, that may not sound like too big of a deal. In New Jersey our yards were very small, about the size of a soccer goal, so when Pamela would tip-toe right to the middle of someone's yard and yank at their flowers, it was probably clear the next morning that someone had taken or eaten the owner's green-thumb treasures.

Pamela was also not afraid to drag other accomplices, meaning ME, to share in her illegal activity. When there was a big bush against a house with flowers too high up, I would get THE LOOK. She'd point the scissors in my direction (yeah, she carried them on the walk) and pleasantly ask, would I go up to the house and destroy the years of care the owner had taken to develop such beautiful landscaping? After that initial question she, of course, would follow up with five minutes of begging and pleading. It would continue until I couldn't handle it anymore, and, sweating in fear, I would tear down flowers from these trees, leaving limbs and a poor example for my kids behind.

Pamela loved fresh flowers and the house was full of them all the time. This is why we always bring fresh flowers to her memorial site. Every time we visit "Mommy's Spot," I look up at that vase and see only stems sticking out. I wonder, did the weather blow the flowers away? Was it the deer that snuck out of the woods and feasted on them? Or just maybe, is it the ghost of one of those homeowners who comes over and yanks the flowers off the stems after we leave the cemetery, in an effort to even the score with Pamela?

Either way, never forget that trespassing and stealing are illegal. Also, never forget what a gracious smile and warm glowing eyes can get someone to do for you when they love you—even if it could get them a healthy fine and 90 days' probation!

CHAPTER ELEVEN

A Lifetime Summed Up in One Word

"Daddy, did you decide what to write on the stone yet?"

Long before I was thrust into the role of widower, I considered what I'd want engraved on my tombstone. Not often, but every couple years I'd think to myself, *How do I want to be remembered?* It's not a bad process to put yourself through. It can motivate you to keep your priorities in balance. In my case, I thought of comical and witty sayings I'd like people to read when visiting my memorial.

"Time Waits For No One,
But I Wouldn't Have Minded A Bit Of A Delay"
or
"Sad As It Is, I'll Never Yell At You Again"

However, when it came to figuring out what to engrave on Pamela's stone, I guess you could say I had writer's block. It wasn't hard to think of all the things I wanted to say, but there's only space for a handful of characters to get your words right, and I don't do well with that kind of pressure. You see, I have what some might say is a flaw but others would call a gift. When you're raised Irish Catholic, from Philadelphia, and your father is a lifetime career salesman by trade, there's one thing you don't have: a loss for words. What you do have is the gift of gab. That kind of upbringing doesn't lend itself to choosing a few words that, once committed, will describe someone for eternity.

What I learned that day and still learn so often from others is that sometimes less is best. I was given a photocopy of the style of stone we'd chosen (oh, yeah, another great decision to make that week) and a short timeframe to decide what the engraving would be. I took it home and showed it to the kids. They were always curious about plans or meetings we had that week, knowing it was all surrounding Pamela but not always appropriate for kids. This time I thought it was a good thing to share. I knew they'd be happy to see there would be carvings of flowers surrounding the border of the memorial stone. I explained we'd put her full name, date of her birth and death, but needed something describing their mom.

Huddled at a corner desk, hands scrunching my forehead I was just giving the paper a blank stare, Kevin Patrick approached from behind me, "Daddy, did you decide what to write on the stone yet?"

I told him I had many ideas but couldn't figure out how to cut it short enough to fit the sixty or so characters I was handcuffed to. He saw that I'd written her name and the dates on the paper, with room below for a tag line that would be her remembrance carved in stone forever.

A few seconds went by. Then Kevin said, "Dad, I know what we should put on it."

I wanted to hear his suggestion, but honestly was a bit worn out and wondering how I'd explain why his idea might not fit.

He said "Mommy".

"Mommy, that was her name, right Daddy?"

I couldn't believe the rush of emotions that raced through my veins. "Oh my God, Kevin, you're right. You know what? If Mommy could have chosen words herself, she probably would have said the very same thing."

There it is: "Mommy."

Pamela Jenks McAteer
May 20, 1970 – February 17, 2007
"Mommy"

....

CHAPTER TWELVE

Legacy

Think about it, and then write your own life obituary. Then go make it come true!

Raleigh—Pamela Jenks McAteer, 36, of Raleigh, died of Leukemia Saturday, February 17, 2007. She is survived by her husband of 10 years, Kevin McAteer; her three small children, sons Kevin Patrick and Christopher, and daughter Amanda. In lieu of flowers, memorials may be made to: Rex Health Care Foundation. Designate funds to the KidsCan! program. KidsCan! was special in Pamela's heart. It is a support group for children with parents who have cancer. Pamela's children had been seeking support through Pamela's illness and treatments. They will continue to reach out to KidsCan! to find strength and help with her loss.

Pamela, You were like no other!
We promise your special caring,
soft touch, and strength to survive
will surround your children
all the days of their lives.
Love always and in our hearts,
Your Neighbors
Your Friends
Your Family
Your Husband

This was the obituary that ran in the *News & Observer* on Tuesday February 20,

2007. It was a chapter I was never supposed to author. I turned page after page at the kitchen table that morning, trying to find the obituary section of the paper to review it in detail and be sure it was correct, since it had the viewing and funeral details listed for visitors.

I sat there completely numb, glaring at the death notices in what I can only describe as a haze of amnesia, thinking to myself, *the press got it wrong. This can't be right.*

Pamela shared the page with eleven other people who had recently passed away. Anyone would have been immediately drawn to her obituary, not only because it was the first one listed, but her photo was one of a stunningly beautiful young woman. That part they got right. What stripped my consciousness of all human logic were the birth dates of the other eleven people:

Ms. Brown—born August 25, 1922
Mr. Douglas "J.D." they called him—born October 26, 1921
Miss Raines—born May 5, 1947
Dr. Williams—born April 12, 1931

The list went on, Ms. Ruby recognized as the oldest at 97 years old. The youngest in that day's line-up other than Pamela was Ms. Price, who lived to be 74 years old.

All I could think was, *What the hell is Pamela doing in this paper? The press had to get it wrong.* Unfortunately the paper didn't get it wrong. Life got it wrong. And for Pamela and her three babies, I wondered what went wrong that our lives deserved such heartache.

Although Pamela's was the first official obituary I'd ever written, I have practiced the art for the past fifteen years. Hers was the first one published but the other fifteen were just as challenging and important for me to write. Those other obituaries were my own.

In my mid-twenties I'd grown attached to reading self-improvement authors, such as Stephen Covey. The most memorable habit I picked up was a very private and introspective way to set personal and professional goals. You hear that goals are important. As an avid sports fan, it's impossible not to replay stories of championship teams claiming that keeping their goals in the forefront of their daily efforts drove them to their pinnacle of success. That all sounded like a reasonable foundation for growth but it also sounded kind of boring. Until I heard a public speaker put this way:

"Close your eyes and imagine for a minute a harsh reality. You have suddenly passed away and you are now having the ghostly experience

of witnessing your own funeral. Think about your life, what you have accomplished; think about those you have touched but also those you have shunned. As you look over the audience attending to pay their respects, who are they, how many are there, is someone missing who you thought would be there? What are they saying about you when they stand up and take the podium? What are they saying about you when huddling in the corner?

Now open your eyes and think about all the important roles in your life. Think about today, and the possibilities of tomorrow. Think about what you hope people will say about you. Think about what you want to be known for.

Think about it, and then write your own life obituary. Then go make it come true!

That's how I started to document my personal, professional, and spiritual life goals some twenty years ago. Each year on my birthday I hide away for a few hours, reflect on my life and then in a very emotional state I theoretically write my own obituary.

After reading Pamela's obituary that dreary Tuesday morning, I questioned if I should hide it away or leave the paper out. I knew the kids would be interested to see Pamela's picture in the paper, but only Kevin Patrick was at an age where he could even stumble through to read it. I decided to leave it out on the table open to the obituary page, figuring I'd let nature take its course. An hour later all three were in awe, spilling Frosted Flakes and milk all over the paper. This was another experience of never knowing what could possibly be going on in a child's head at that young age. Kevin Patrick attempted to read it word for word. Amanda was actually joyful because she noticed her name was listed in the paper. It gave her a feeling of pride that she and Mommy were in the paper together. Then Christopher immediately pulled and tugged at the paper, hoping he'd see his awfully difficult, lengthy name in lights. When he did, he was at peace that he wasn't forgotten. Who in their wildest imagination would have predicted that three kids under the age of six would see an obituary of their mom, who'd passed away only days earlier, and find peace and joy to have their names listed in the same ink that announced the most tragic moment of their lifetime?

What would motivate someone to read and want to hear more? I had no idea, until that obituary moved a mother expecting her third child to call me a few days later. That mother was also a reporter for the *News & Observer*.

Bonnie called my house many times, leaving several messages on our voicemail. Finally, one day when I walked into the kitchen my mom handed me the daily list of messages and voicemails she'd screened for me, with Bonnie's name and number again listed. Mom said, "She's going to keep calling until you respond," so I mustered some patience, of which I had very little for anyone but the kids, and dialed her number.

Bonnie was a writer who documented life stories each week for the *News and Observer*. It was her practice to review obituaries in an effort to find someone who may have touched others' lives in a unique way. When she came upon Pamela's, the first thing that caught her eye was how young Pamela was. Then to read about how many young children she left behind and an apparent loving husband was very moving. What also seemed worthy of digging deeper was the interest in this KidsCan! organization. She was confident there was a story worth writing about.

When we finally talked the conversation was somewhat brief and, as Bonnie describes it, quite shocking. First, she was surprised I finally called her back and agreed to meet with her. She'd assumed there was a pretty good chance I'd deny having the strength, time, or fortitude to include her in my daily schedule. The second surprise was that I was willing to invite her to our home, a place so raw in heartbreak due to our great loss. I had limited experience at working with the press, but enough to know what they write in the end is entirely their privilege. I felt a bit vulnerable for more reasons than one. By asking Bonnie to meet us at Brookfield Road, I was leveling the playing field a bit.

At this stage I knew Bonnie's goal in general, but I was extremely hesitant about opening up to her and allowing her to write an article about Pamela and our family. However, I had blind trust in the idea behind the story and what it might mean to KidsCan!. Just as important, it could become a documented journal of Pamela's life for the kids to use as a source of recollection. But I wasn't dealing with an author wanting to create a documentary or life memoir. I was dealing with a reporter who worked for a newspaper. I was anxious that I might get fooled or she might not be morally aligned with us as a family. When Bonnie first walked through the door, I was a bit more settled. Maybe it was due to her nervous demeanor; or was it the way she carried a huge basketball in her undeniably pregnant tummy, barely squeezing through our front door?

I wanted to be prepared for what I felt was a showdown with the press. The whole idea of talking to a reporter weeks after my wife's passing felt so odd to me, yet I also felt a type of calling, compelled by my love and devotion. In the end my instincts remained on guard. I'd made sure I had plenty of help and a game plan to sneak away quietly to my neighbor's house for the interview. My mom and Christina, our recently appointed nanny, watched the kids to avoid their otherwise outpouring of love and appreciation to any stranger who stopped by to pay their respects. This could throw me a curve ball from the interrogation tactics I'd planned for Bonnie. I had a list of questions prepared, as if I were the reporter.

When Bonnie came in, she met Mom and Christina, and then we sat down alone. I was nervous about how I might react to the conversation. I knew, as my mom did, that my temperament was fragile. I was worried I'd grow tired of the process after a few questions, then brush Bonnie off or even act indifferent towards her. If this conversation started out on the wrong foot it would end quickly. I hoped that I would be impressed with her sincerity about my family, and wanting to honestly tell a short story of the woman and mother we all adored, so I had some memories already typed out on paper.

I was surprised that as the discussion began Bonnie didn't know exactly what she was going to write about. She explained to me later that she knew there was a story here, but hadn't figured out yet what made it unique or compelling.

Bonnie recalls being equally nervous about meeting me, but of course for very different reasons. Her nerves came from a very personal place, as well. She'd later admit it was one of the most emotional moments in her career. She said as a journalist you have to try to stay neutral and not get too tied up in the despair someone experiences as they tell their story. However, as a pregnant mother and near Pamela's age, the entire scene was saddening.

As we toured the house to show her family photos hung in each room, Bonnie froze in her tracks when she spotted a large basket of LEGO toys on the floor. I'd reminisced about play dates where mothers would ask, "Where's Pamela?" to then find her on the floor, helping the kids build the best amateur-engineered LEGO tower possible. We were heading outside through the laundry room door when I caught sight of one of Pamela's most ingenious trademarks. I called it Pamela's "dentist basket." She kept a wicker basket of dollar store toys for those days when an unexpected child would visit, or when bribery was necessary to buy some peace from the kids. Normally a mom would reserve McDonald's for those times, but there were days when dragging three toddlers into the fun-bus (otherwise known as the family van) was too overwhelming a task, considering the remaining motherly energy left in her gas tank. I felt as if I were sharing a lesson from Nostradamus. Bonnie was receiving a privately passed on legacy through the lens of one wise mom to another. At this point I was confident she was more than qualified for this gift of survival advice, although to Bonnie it was more like sharing a love story.

I didn't think spending any more time spilling tears on the McAteer grounds was needed, so we agreed I'd meet her at a local bagel shop later that week to share some photos for the article. I asked Kevin Patrick to join me, knowing he'd be interested in meeting a real-life reporter. I couldn't keep what I was doing with Bonnie a secret from the kids, so I thought it would inspire him to know his mom was so important to the world that the local newspaper, the same one that covered his favorite professional baseball team and would write about Hollywood movies, would also feature Pamela McAteer's story. Bonnie later summarized her reaction to the bagel shop meeting as one of amazement. How could this father and son smile at life when it had taken such a wrong turn? It brought her back to that dining room table where she described me as appearing to "have it together" and actually being upbeat, though we were both bawling at times and sharing moments of searing pain. She'd assumed meeting the McAteers during those weeks would be a picture of total despair and hopelessness.

Meeting the kids and me she saw how tight a family unit we were, especially for a group of loved ones who suddenly had to live with a deep void that most likely would never be totally filled again. Bonnie describes it as an act of character that we were inwardly and outwardly still such a loving and inspiring family.

Bonnie had opened her heart and pen to me and I felt at peace as we finished our time together. She was racing toward a deadline in hopes to get the article ready for the upcoming May 13th Mother's Day Sunday edition. She explained to me that it's up to the Senior Editor when the article runs in the paper, and she'd have no way of knowing until the day before if the paper, in fact, would carry her story in the Sunday Journal Section of the newspaper.

Bonnie contacted me the day before Mother's Day, telling me the early decision was not to run it on that day, but certainly to run it within the next couple weeks, and definitely in the Sunday edition. Her call was a relief. Hearing it was not going to print on Mother's Day meant I didn't have to worry about the horror that might creep into my consciousness when second guessing my decision on an already difficult holiday for everyone.

A week later I got a voicemail from Bonnie that she was fairly confident the article would be printed in the May 20th Sunday edition. May 20th was Pamela's birthday, a date entirely unscripted by the paper since they didn't even know her birth date was falling on a Sunday. In one respect I was happy it would be published on this day. If it was well received, it would be a tribute to Pamela on her actual birthday. However, if it was something to regret, the weight I'd carry would be crippling. Pamela shares the same birthday as her older brother Chris, who was in town specifically to not celebrate but to be there for his mom and the kids, on what he knew would be a rough day for all of us as well as for him.

May 20, 2007, I woke up around 5:30 am and quietly made my way outside in hopes to be the first one in Raleigh to get the *News & Observer* that morning. On my way up the driveway I thought, *Maybe they pulled the story at the last minute. Ah, that would be okay; this day is tough enough. I don't need the added intensity.* As I approached the rolled-up paper, my mind continued to wonder. *How meaningful it would be to have the story on her birthday, even more than Mother's Day, since fewer call this date their special day.* As I picked the newspaper up off the cold cement I wondered if I'd even be able to find the story in the tons of pages of the thick Sunday edition. All that second guessing never prepared me for what happened when I unrolled the paper, standing all alone at the top of our long driveway.

My heart sank.

In the top right-hand corner above the day's top headline was a color photo of one-and-a-half year-old little Christopher in my arms as I stood beside the kitchen sink, looking into the beautiful, innocent face of this motherless baby boy, the photo showing Christopher's hands playfully patting my cheeks in an almost intended message of "Daddy, it will be alright."

I knew participating in the article would be a decision I would be happy about, but I also did my best to prepare for disappointment. However, I was not ready to see Christopher and me in color for the three hundred thousand readers who'd peek at the Sunday front page that day.

The walk back down the driveway was supposed to have been one of curiosity, wondering how many pages of black ink would be on my thumb before finding the story. Instead I felt like Jesus with splinters covering His back from carrying the cross, praying that someone would take it from me, but knowing I had to be the one to carry this weight. That crippled emotion I had not felt with such intensity since walking down the aisle of a church behind the casket carrying my wife. That weight I'd put aside now reminded me with one newspaper photo, this was my life; it was my reality.

I quickly walked to the kitchen table in hopes of reading the entire article before the kids woke up and, more importantly, before Pamela's mom and brother read it. What was supposed to take minutes to find, I'd found in three seconds. On the front page of the Life Journal Section of the *News & Observer* was another 8 by 10 color photo of us, and others of Pamela on her hospital bed with Amanda. The headline read "When Mommy is Very Sick—Helping Children Cope." I'll never be able to explain why at that moment I was drowning in regret. I read every word and buried my face in my hands. Soaking with tears my fingers flipped through looking at the pictures of then and now of my family, I had only one thought: *I just made the biggest mistake of my life.* I could not find a single word or sentence that made me proud of my decision, made me pleased to have ever met Bonnie

As I finished the article, that covered two full pages of news real estate, my first thought was of Lyn and Chris. How upset they would be? And how dreadful that a little later I was supposed to come over to their house with the kids, so we could go to church together. All I could think of was, *Life has been hell for all of us, getting by one morning at a time, and I have just taken our life misery and graffitied the community paper with our story. A community that has done everything they could for both Lyn and the kids to put us on their shoulders.* Then I thought of the children. I was so happy they couldn't read the article, although I knew I couldn't hide what their father had done. As they came down the stairs, I left the paper on the table open to the full-page article about their mother, hoping the photos and the recognition of their names in ink would be all they needed. Thankfully, I was right. The kids did ask me to help them find their names and anyone else mentioned. At one point they wanted me to read the article but I just couldn't. I was not ready for their reaction, not until I faced Lyn and Chris to apologize.

A few hours later we pulled into Lyn's driveway. I'd dodged having any conversation with her earlier that morning, having the kids talk to them on the phone to confirm what time we'd pick them up for church. I was so upset I didn't even want to walk in their front door. *Why did I add to this woman's burden?* Then I mustered up the guts to go in and take my punishment for the lousy choices I'd made.

Walking into the house, I probably felt the same as Bonnie felt meeting me that first day. My intentions were good, but I was scared to death. Lyn came down the stairs in her typical upbeat mood, but you could see a slight disguising of the harsh reality that today was a day she should be celebrating with her daughter, not remembering her. As she was attacked with a hug from one of the kids, I had to get it out.

"Did you see the paper this morning?"

"Yes. I thought it was beautiful."

"What? Really, Lyn?"

"Yes, I am so proud that you did that. It must have been so hard for you, but what a tribute to Pamela"

I felt I'd been dropped into someone else's life. I wanted to fall to my knees in mental exhaustion: "Lyn, you just changed my whole life. For the first time since Pamela got sick, I regretted the choices I made. I had no idea how I was going to carry on today, or this week, after I read that article that seemed unethical as a father and immoral as a husband to have agreed to be written."

Chris came down minutes later. I was only half relieved to hear Lyn's reaction but I knew if Chris felt the same way, then I'd totally misread the outcome of the tearful efforts Bonnie and I had put towards sharing our life story. Chris, whom I respect mostly for his honesty, even when his position is not the majority, agreed with Lyn.

As I said, I can't explain it, because I haven't read the story again since that morning and probably never will. I know the story gave every detail of what Pamela had to overcome, gave every experience of what we as parents went through, and didn't miss any important joyful or sad outcome for the entire family. I know the article was written in a manner that every detail, every answer to any question the children might have of those 12 months, was answered. I didn't realize at the time that not only was it a tribute to Pamela, but it would be the vehicle for tens of thousands of dollars in donations to the KidsCan! program in her name.

Through the uncertainty, I convinced myself that my personal opinion of the article didn't matter. As long as it didn't hurt the kids or Lyn and it changed one life, one family, one parent, then I did Pamela proud taking the risk of meeting with Bonnie. I wonder sometimes, if my resolve had been different would the story have been written?

It was interesting to talk to Bonnie four years later and hear her recollection of our working on this story together. Her article went to print almost 100 days after Pamela's death, but also less than 30 days from Bonnie giving birth to her third child. That made it a bit too painful for her to go back and reread what she'd written, since it took so much out of her at that time in her life. Bonnie explained what many people experienced during that time, there's always that one moment of human weakness when we say to ourselves, "Oh, my God, if this could happen to this family, it could happen to anyone, to me."

What made Bonnie's pen and Pamela's life so inspiring and shocking was that as people read our story, they waited for what seemed the obvious ending. The same ending Pamela and I thought was obvious too, she'd beat cancer! To family, friends and the loyal readers of the *News & Observer* it was shattering to reach the end of the story and discover she'd died. Thanks to one mom's powerful ability to write, and another's to live even in the face of death, Pamela's legacy was able to be captured in black and white.

It was in Pamela's passing that her story was told, but it was when she lived that many of us started to record it. That was evident from a phone conversation I had with her best friend from when we lived in Maplewood, New Jersey. Months and months after the funeral, Kirsten and I finally had a chance to talk one night. Kirsten, like Pamela, was a busy mom with two kids around the same ages. Coincidentally, her husband John also worked in the hotel business, as I do. She reminisced about how amazed she always was with Pamela's daily outlook on life, her positive attitude and her willingness—no matter how exhausted they both were—to make life special for the kids. She always loved sharing the story of the indoor pool Pamela created in our basement one day when both of them were venting about the crappy weather outside. They had the kids trapped in the house all day and chores that needed to be done, and husbands that had to work late. It was Pamela's idea to invite Kirsten over to the house with Jack and Katie for a play date. What Kirsten didn't know was why she needed them to bring their bathing suits on a cold, rainy day in New Jersey. Neither did I until I came down the stairs from work that night looking for everyone. What I found in my "man cave" was a medium-sized kid's pool filled in my basement. This was the last place in the house I could claim as my own. Needless to say, I was shocked at the indoor swimming facility Pamela opened that day for Kirsten and the kids. I was not shocked that she'd never thought about how she'd pick up and move 55 gallons of water to empty the pool in a sink. That was Pamela.

However, the real defining moment of that conversation with Kirsten was this quote: "I try so hard when life is busy and the kids are begging for time I don't have, to ask myself: *What would Pamela do right now?* She'd always find a way to be cool, calm, and collected and make sure the top priority for the day was loving and engaging with our kids. She could always find humor in the little ones who cause so much stress, and see the beauty in the simple things each day. Kevin, I just can't live up to it. I so much want to be more like her in honor of her, but it's just too hard. I'll never meet someone so special again."

Caring so much about their family and their unwavering support for Pamela and me, I gave Kirsten the best advice I could: "Kirsten, what you need to do is simple. Go buy a large inflatable children's pool, at least able to hold 60 gallons, fill it up, and surround it with bags of play-sand and show John just how much I miss him. Don't forget to send me pictures of his Yankees Man Cave turned into the beach-front pool area he and you deserve!"

Bonnie put Pamela's legacy to me in two simple words: "A smile."

CHAPTER THIRTEEN

When LEGO Bricks are Not a Boy's Best Friend

*"Kevin, I need you to come home, I need you now.
Kevin Patrick is stuck, and I can't get him out!"*

I don't think I will ever erase the memory of the day I was speeding home to rescue Kevin Patrick, from the most unsuspecting danger, his mother. We lived in New Jersey at the time and I'd just started my 45-minute commute from work when I got a call from Pamela. I'd never heard her voice this way before, crying/laughing/choking/yelling all at the same time.

"What the heck is going on?" I yelled.

Now laughing hysterically, Pamela said, "Kevin, I need you to come help me. Kevin Patrick is stuck, and I can't get him out!"

I was in a panic, "Oh my God Pamela, where is he stuck?"

"In the middle of the LEGO table your mom bought him. He's naked, crying and stuck in the center of it."

What do you ask first? "Why is my three-year-old naked and why would he try to fit himself in the middle opening of a children's play table?" Or do I dare ask, "How long has he been there?" I went with the second one, and regret it to this day.

"He's been in there awhile. When I found him I couldn't stop laughing and had to get the camera to take pictures, so maybe a half hour or longer he's been stuck."

I pressed harder on the gas pedal, out of frustration but also out of urgency to save my firstborn from his crazy mother. As I neared the highway exit I gave her a few suggestions: "Dump baby powder where his skin is sticking to the plastic siding. Or see if you can get some Vaseline between him and the side of the hole."

Then I hung up. I couldn't handle her laugh, or her desperate tears, and—more importantly—Kevin Patrick's cry for help in the background.

As I burst through the front door like a SWAT team, there they were. Kevin stark naked, still trapped in the middle of a LEGO table with powder stuck all over him, with a red rash developing around his hips. Pamela sat on the floor with her well-known ear-to-ear smile. Tears streamed down both their faces, hers from laughing so hard, his from the onslaught of unjustified torture. Quickly assessing the situation, I sprang into action.

"Pamela, go get me a beer."

"Kevin Patrick, this may hurt, but you'll be out in a few seconds."

I applied more powder, braced the table, reached under his arms, and quickly pulled upward, praying his penis would not get chopped off in the aggressive rescue move. Quickly, I had Kevin Patrick safely in my arms. Unfortunately, the table was still hanging from his waist.

After a few minutes and a few sips of my beer, I was able to wiggle him to freedom. As much as I could have pummeled her, I'll always be grateful for the photos Pamela took of Kevin Patrick in that LEGO table!

Grandma McAteer, I have to say, "Best gift everrrrrrrr."

CHAPTER FOURTEEN

Not One Loss is the Same

"We will love differently, we will grieve differently,
we will hurt differently, and we will remember differently."

Loss can bring on judgment and it can also turn some people into instant advice column specialists.

One night our door bell rang. It was unusual to get an unannounced visitor after the kid's bedtime. It was a mom whose child was in one of my kids' classes. The family had suffered a similar loss a few years earlier.

"I'm here for you. Know you can call me if you ever need anything, or just need someone to lend an ear. I've been there and know how hard it was to get where I am today."

About 35 minutes later the woman finally stopped talking, and stopped reminding me she was there to listen. To have loved and learned, to have lost and lived again can be one of life's toughest but most helpful experiences.

Handing off those lessons to others in similar situations at times can lessen their suffering. However, each year in America about 600,000 people pass away from cancer and more than 900,000 marriages end in divorce; not a single one is the same. It's true that I did learn from others with young children who lost a spouse, or their life experience helped me shape my own healing process and gave me knowledge about how to make the best decisions for me and the kids. But no matter how similar another family's loss, each will be a unique situation. We will love differently, we will grieve differently, we will hurt differently, and we will remember differently.

Share your loss, share what helped you get through, and even share what seemed like good advice but was of no use to you in the end. Often I'm asked if I'd be a sounding board for another father or family thrown into a life altering adversity. I always say yes, thinking, *I made it; I can help them, too.* I tell the friend of the person who's in pain to have them call me, e-mail me, leave me a voice mail at work, whatever is most comfortable for them.

People who are grieving will call, when they're ready. Don't reach out to them unless they ask you to. And when someone reaches out for help, spend most of your time really listening. When I do get that call to visit a family who is hurting I only take a minute to express my story to them:

"I'd be happy to share what my loss was like and what resources helped me and taught me, but each of our situations are unique, so tell me how you're feeling and how I can help. And if you don't mind, I'll just listen and think of where, how, or who can help you find your answers. I experienced a lot and learned a lot from my loss and from others' who had awful loss, but I honestly can't answer for you how I made it. I really don't know. I just know that I did."

....

CHAPTER FIFTEEN

The UPS Man

"I have to tell you how much your wife has meant to me."
Not what a husband wants to hear from the mailman.

One of the most powerful stories I will ever tell about Pamela involves a UPS man who for a short time in 2007 had our home on his mail route.

Those who knew her well would first think this story has to do with the many UPS boxes that showed up at the house unexpectedly, from Lillian Vernon and many other retail on-line stores. After I'd go to bed, Pamela would pull out catalogues she got in the mail and order new personalized knick-knacks and gifts for all of us. Every time a box would show up I'd shake my head. However, I could never get mad at her because like Grandma McAteer, Pamela almost always shopped for others and not for herself (except, of course, when it came to in-mall shoe shopping). Some of the best gifts we've ever received, some of the warmest items in our home, are from her late night catalogue shopping excursions.

About a month after Pamela passed away, the final family members left the house to let the four of us begin the journey of finding our way. One early evening, after putting dinner on the table for the three children, I walked up the driveway to get the mail. We have to be careful at our mailbox because cars on the road can come very close. As I pulled the mail out, I suddenly jumped because a large brown UPS truck pulled almost right against me. During those days it was not unusual to get a UPS care package from someone in the family. So I turned, expecting a delivery.

The UPS driver popped out (I wish I remembered his name). I'd never seen him before, yet he walked right up to me with a serious look on his face and said, "I just had to introduce myself and tell you how sorry I am for your loss, and make sure you're doing okay." I thanked him, figuring he knew Pamela from the many secret deliveries I never knew about. But he stopped me in my tracks in a way I didn't expect.

He froze me by saying, "I have to tell you something about your wife and how much she's meant to me." Not what a husband wants to hear from a mailman. But he continued his story by telling me he'd driven a UPS truck for almost 30 years, in many different cities throughout the county, from Los Angeles to Detroit, and the last several years in Raleigh. He was not our regular driver but was given this route for a few months until a new driver picked the route up. He then gave me "the UPS driver outlook on life."

He said "You know, doing this for a living I see all kinds of things at people's homes, I see all kind of families, all kind of parents and how they take care of their kids. I've driven in bad neighborhoods and often nice neighborhoods like this one. The thing about these nice neighborhoods is that the homes are beautiful and have a great façade on the outside, but on the inside I rarely see a beautiful neighborhood. I see moms and dads and how they live, rarely reflecting a home full of love and laughter. But that all changed for me when I got this route. I'm sure you know how special your wife was," he continued. "But I thought you should know from a perfect stranger how special she was to someone like me, and how she has changed my life.

"I'd never had a delivery for your house but always noticed it when delivering to nearby homes. It caught my eye that almost every time I passed your house I would see this mom outside with these three kids, blowing bubbles, or playing ball, or just running around having fun. Sometimes it was so active there seemed to be five or six kids. I would see this motherly, playful love, the kind of beauty that should be in a neighborhood that looks this good, matching the outside façade. Finally I just had to stop and speak to her.

"I parked my truck and walked down the driveway, as once again the four of them played outside together. She turned and walked towards me and greeted me with such a warm, happy smile. I began to explain, 'I'm sorry for interrupting you and unfortunately I don't have a package for you, but I just had to meet you.'" He went on to tell her his experience of watching her every day and it just overtook him that he had to meet this mom and tell her how unusual she was to always find the time and energy, especially with three little kids, to play and have fun with them.

His story really hit home about Pamela when he said, "You know what really blows me away? That day I stopped to say hi, she not only was warm and friendly but talked to me for what felt like an hour. As her kids ran around her, she gave me such attention that she made me—a perfect stranger, just a UPS guy—feel like the most important person in her life at that moment. Finally I realized I was taking her away from the very thing that drove me to meet her, her kids, so I said goodbye to all of them and went on my way.

"After that day, I'd stop once in a while and say hi to her and the kids from the truck. As weeks went on I had some deliveries for your mother-in-law down the street, and that's how I learned your wife was sick. Of course, I'd still see her from time to time playing with the kids in the yard, even as she was battling cancer. Finally one day I had a package for the McAteers and looked forward to going to your front door. I rang the doorbell and your oldest son came charging to the door. 'How is your mommy feeling?' I asked. 'My Mommy died,' he said. I thought the boy was joking at first and said, 'What do you mean? That's not funny.' He told me he wasn't joking. 'My Mommy died a few weeks ago.' At that moment a family member came to the door to take the package and gave me the rest of the news.

"Mr. McAteer, it's been weeks now and I still can't shake the news your son gave me that day. Your wife changed my outlook and hopes for this country, this world, when I was beginning to have serious doubts. I want you to know I think of you every day and how special a person she was, not just an incredible mom but what a wonderful person to make me, a perfect stranger, feel so important when she had so much more to do at that time."

Of course I already knew everything the UPS driver told me. But I never heard the story of Pamela from a perfect stranger. Pamela was the most caring mother/person/neighbor/worker/human being. It didn't matter if she'd met you before, or you were her friend, rich or poor, young or old. She had the ability to make anyone feel they were the most important person to her at that time.

The UPS driver asked me if it would be okay to stop by sometime with gifts or goodies for the three children. He said he wouldn't bother us, but drop it by the door in the next few days or over the upcoming weekend. "Of course" I said, "that would be no problem."

As he pulled his truck away, passing inches from me and the mailbox, I took only a few steps before crying my eyes out as I walked slowly toward the house. Yes, I cried out of sadness Pamela wasn't here, but also because I was so happy and proud to say the person he'd just talked to me about was my wife, the love of my life, and mom of my children.

His story was so moving that day, and his sincerity so strong I thought for sure he would drop off a care package. But I never saw him again.

Apparently a new driver got the route soon after our meeting by the mailbox. Sometimes I daydream that he never came back because he was an angel disguised as a UPS driver, sent to remind me it was time, now that all our family had left, to figure out how I was going to handle raising the three children on my own. He was sent to remind me that in the end it's all about living in the moment.

That angel dressed like a UPS driver did deliver a gift to the kids. Only it didn't come in a brown box, it came in a story. The gift was to never forget the most important thing Pamela taught all of us. Live in the moment, love and laugh in the moment, and always care about blowing bubbles!

CHAPTER SIXTEEN

Only Two Words in Spanish

What she taught me, and what she instilled in my children can be summed up in two words.

In my senior year in high school I took a Spanish class. I don't recall my grade but it was somewhere between an A and an F. Years later, in college, I elected to take Spanish again and did okay, probably around a B-minus. After working six months in a Florida hotel, surrounded by co-workers who spoke Spanish as a first language, I started to pick up the lingo; at least enough to get me through a day of being teased for my rough translations as we pumped out hundreds of burgers for the tourists in our restaurant.

After my internship in Florida I headed back to my senior year of college. I figured I'd done well enough in both the classroom and real life—using and speaking Spanish—that I might as well take Spanish II, a more advanced class. I expected this would be an easy class to help my GPA as I closed out my college career. I was wrong.

My father likes to brag that he graduated college with a minor in Spanish. In my third year of Spanish classes, none of that *mojo* helped me in the least. I was spiraling into failing my first college course. As soon as Spanish was no longer part of my everyday eight-hour work shift, it was no longer as natural as flipping hamburger patties.

I should have figured out I wasn't going to get to continue to practice my Spanish street smack at a liberal arts college in Erie, Pennsylvania. Luckily I found a small window of opportunity to pass the class and not embarrass myself or, especially, my father. I was heading into finals week of my last semester of college, so I don't think my parents cared what my grade was, as long as it didn't stop me from graduating. For that reason I decided not to share that "window of opportunity" with them. Let's just say when eight of your football teammates are in the same class, all failing as miserably as you, and you hear the teacher could use cheap labor to paint his large, three-story house, you kind of lean on your decent grades from business administration. Yeah, that's right. The eight of us never took the final exam. Instead, we spent two days painting and drinking our Corona. And guess what? Yep. We passed. Just passed, but pass we did.

After college I went into complete Spanish amnesia. The only phrases I remembered were *Buenos dias* (Good day) and *Mucho cerveza* (More beer). That was until I met a great teacher, and a beautiful guardian angel. Yes, that best describes Christina (although the name is so common I think I should just follow the trend of not including folks first names in the book), the wonderful nanny we hired the week Pamela went back in the hospital, after falling out of remission.

Before I share with you the two unforgettable words my new nanny/Spanish professor taught me, you first should know how Christina fits in our history. Once we understood how difficult Pamela's battle against leukemia was going to be the second time around, she and I decided to hire full-time child care. First, I needed help to hang onto my job at Concord, and second, it was going to be a necessity once Pamela made it through chemo treatments and then a bone marrow trans-plant. The transplant would put her at least a hundred days away from being fully able to care for herself, let alone the three kids.

Pamela raced to interview people within the seven-day window Dr. Crane gave her before her trip back to the cancer treatment floor at Rex. I could have been a bigger help, but felt she was going to suffer so much not being able to help the kids daily that if she chose the person to care for them, there'd be less chance she'd grow jealous of another woman playing her motherly role. She screened potential nannies on the phone, invited them to the house, and I dilly dallied around doing mindless chores so she could get a read on whether the person was strong enough to handle the kids, not to mention care for a young woman fighting daily to regain her moth-erhood. If someone seemed to pass the test, I'd join in to make sure I had chemistry with her. I also wanted to know she'd be able to help manage the house and not just be someone with a glowing personality like Pamela's. We needed a manager but also a caregiver and nurturer. I had to be cautious that we didn't hire someone who felt right just because they'd grown fond of one another in a few quick minutes.

We really struggled. Most of the women were so young we didn't think they could handle both roles of warden with the kids and co-manager of the home. It was eye-opening that a few we wanted to hire never called back. Perhaps the emo-tional burden of compassion for a woman near their age who was so heart-wrench-ingly sick was too much.

We'd hoped to hire someone before Pamela checked into Rex on that Saturday morning, but we hadn't been able to land on the right person. There was one more possibility, a woman referred to us by a friend. Pamela heard everything she wanted to hear about Christina, things she'd not heard with any other applicant. Christina was older, although she never shared her age with us. She was the middle sibling from a family of thirteen kids, so she knew about big families. She was single, living nearby with her son and daughter who were attending high school and college locally. Pamela's friend who recommended Christina had two pretty rambunctious boys, so we knew she could handle the energy of our three.

It seemed she had it all, a young spirit, the work ethic of a hard laborer, experience as a mother, the sense of how brothers and sisters grow up together. And she knew what cancer can do to a family, because she'd lost her sister to cancer. Where she was from in Columbia, the medical treatment was nowhere near what it is in the U.S., so it's difficult to tell what kind of cancer struck her sister or whether it was curable, but she thought it had been leukemia. What resonated most with us was Christina's sharing how her sister left behind a young daughter who had no father to speak of, so Christina and other members of their family raised the daughter while dealing with the sorrow of a lost sibling and lost mother.

Pamela decided that while she was still in the hospital dealing with chemo treatments, she'd have Christina work a half day at our home. I guess with that résumé it seemed a no brainer to Pamela, and if the three kids and I liked her after spending a few hours together, then all that was left in the interview process was a quick visit with Pamela at the hospital so they could meet face to face. That's exactly what happened.

We had a great afternoon with Christina. She was the perfect blend of the strict teacher you always loved in school who made sure you followed the rules, the enthusiasm of a twenty-year-old woman working in day care for the first time, and the most detailed housekeeper I'd ever seen, including the thousands who had worked in my hotels over the previous fifteen years.

Pamela and Christina met privately at Rex Hospital on Thursday of that week, the day before Pamela was supposed to come home. Christina was on board and officially now a part of our family. She was to start at 8 a.m. Monday morning.

Christina never made it into work that first day, because Pamela never made it home from the hospital. I asked my father to call Christina to tell her not to bother driving out on Monday, but that I would desperately need her help if she was still interested. She was to come by on Tuesday just to say hi to the kids for a few hours, but she was determined to officially start her full-time work helping us put the pieces back together of our lives, to do whatever it took to get the kids and me through our tragic loss.

I often think back and wonder: *Wow, can you imagine being Christina, showering one morning, sitting down with a cup of coffee to organize your week around the start of a new job, then to get a call from someone you've never met saying, "Your boss is no longer alive. We won't need you on Monday"?*

I can't imagine her response to my father. I can't imagine what she would say to the kids. I wonder what she and Pamela talked about during that one chance they had to meet, days before Pamela's passing, and Christina's entering our lives. All I know is what Christina did say, what she taught me, and what she instilled in my children. It can be summed up in two words that will resonate with me every day, especially when trouble comes my way. BE HAPPY!

I know it sounds simple, but this Columbian angel with her thick, charming accent had gifted our family with two simple words and a smile that lit up her face every time she said, "Be Happy!"

At first I found these two words a bit odd to hear each morning as I went off to work. Normally someone would say, "Bye, Mr. McAteer" or "Have a good day." It was also unusual because the morning was the one time I was outwardly happy. I'm an energetic morning person by nature, and most positive in the early hours of the day. The other reason I'd almost skip to the car in the morning was knowing Christina was about to arrive down the driveway. This meant I was going to be at work in 10-15 minutes. At that time in my single parent experience, the office became a place to relax and not feel worn by the constant parenting role of non-stop cleaning up, answering questions, and coaching behaviors. There was nothing more fulfilling than hearing the kids say, "Bye Daddy. See you after work. We love you." Yet still, every single day when I saw her before floating off to my job, she'd make sure to say, "BE HAPPY!"

I laugh at this Spanish lesson of how to live life. Even more amusing are the stories I hear from the kids about their time with Christina. First, I'll say that Amanda loved Christina, for all the attention she gave her as a little girl and for being a daily female role model in her mom's absence. Christina adored Christopher and he easily returned her unselfish caring with his sensitive appreciation of hand holding and hugs. Kevin Patrick, on the other hand, gave her a run for her money. I think he liked and respected her, but as a part of the grieving process hated that his mom was not at home to teach him right from wrong, help him with his homework, and all the other ways parents nurture their children.

Christina didn't have it easy helping us. She would rush from the other side of town early in the morning, trying to beat traffic, help drive the kids to school, clean up the house, do the laundry, run between the folding of laundry to pick up the little ones from school, feed them dinner, pack lunches for the next day, and finally do everything she could to pick up so the house was welcoming for my arrival home. At the same time, we did struggle through a bit of a language barrier. She and I were both so busy, days could go by when all we did was hustle past each other in the driveway, one of us getting in a car, the other rushing out of a car. This meant I often had to communicate with her by leaving notes each day. I didn't realize her gift of gab in English didn't cross over to *reading* English. Only later did I learn she was still a little shaky at reading English, and would ask her kids to translate our notes while helping them with transportation to school or night jobs.

One day when I was driving the kids to McDonald's for an early Saturday breakfast treat, I was at a stop light and needed to text someone on my cell phone (I don't do that while driving, but when I'm at a light it's *game on*). I was the first one at the light so I said to the kids, "Someone let me know when the light turns green so I can look up, stop texting, and start driving." Together they responded, "Dad, we can do that, no problem. We used to do that for Christina all the time when she closed her eyes to rest at red lights on the way to school. We'd yell, "GREEENNNNN" to wake her up so she could drive."

After her long day with my kids, heading off at 6 pm to start her second job of being a parent of two young adults, no matter what difficulties the day had brought, the last thing I'd hear from Christina was, "BE HAPPY, gooodd night, Mcateersss." I guess going to her next job, like me in the morning, felt like relaxation compared to the care of three motherless young children.

These days when I catch myself saying "Be happy," I think back to those early days and wonder, *Did Christina have the intuition to say those two words because, although I looked happy on the outside, she knew I wasn't ready to be happy on the inside?*

I've heard it takes a person almost twenty consecutive days to make something a natural behavior, make it a habit. I'm not sure how accurate that is, but I can say it took about twenty months of Christina caring for our family to make it a habit for me to say, "Be happy." I don't say it every day, but I do find it's instinctive for me when I know someone is having a tough time. When I can't seem to find the right words for a friend or co-worker facing adversity I'll sign off a card or email with "Be happy." I love to say it to my kids after they've had a rough morning with their siblings, or at night when we aren't all getting along.

With my horrible imitation of a Columbian accent, it sounds like "BEahh HAPPee." Although it will never get me an acting job on the Spanish soap opera channel, I know it's a subtle reminder of Christina to my kids, of what she did for us, what she meant to our family, and that although life can be tough, we can lift spirits and give hope with the translation of the loving and caring *Se Feliz*: "BE HAPPY!"

....

CHAPTER SEVENTEEN

Faces

The face of that father has never been the same.

In those last moments in the ICU room alone next to Pamela's bed, I made a few promises. The most important was finishing raising our kids in the most loving environment possible. At the time those were just words, words I was honestly not ready to back up as I was numb with grief and disbelief. I didn't know I would take the baton starting at 6 am the day after her death. The first morning I woke up a widower I wasn't ready to look in the mirror, so the mirror came to me. I barely cleared my vision when I saw my reflection in that mirror, a reflection within a set of powder blue eyes of a four-year-old little girl.

I learned years later and still have to manage today, that my process of mourning and healing has had many different faces. The moment the doctors and nurses stopped scurrying around the hospital bed and the beeping of medical equipment ceased, I suffered the most life-altering, unrealistic loss of my life. I lost my wife and my best friend. It wasn't until thirty minutes later, that I realized the next tragedy. Our children had no idea their Mommy wasn't going to be driving next to me in the passenger seat. I was broken; I had just lost the mother of my children and was drowning in grief.

Then and still today I mourn the loss of their mother. When raising them becomes a mountain of adversity or a test of exhaustion, I selfishly grieve the loss of my trusted, nurturing partner, who was to be by my side at every turn in raising the kids.

When I do have the strength to muscle the demands of fatherhood, I'm faced with an even greater step in the process—handling the unfairness of the ever growing mountain of precious moments Pamela has lost out on:

Not standing on the asphalt, weeping, as Christopher's warm hand separates from hers on his first day of Kindergarten.

Missing the enthusiasm of accomplishment in Amanda's face the first time she comes down stairs to show how well she can do her own ponytails. Even if one is hanging from the top of her head.

Never watching with pride as Kevin Patrick catches his first touchdown pass.

I don't argue with others when they say, unsolicited, how strong a father figure I am for my three children. I know I am. I know I've not let Pamela down. Yet I also know that now at the end of a work day it's not the same man exiting the car when Kevin Patrick, Amanda and Christopher run outside screaming, "Daddy's home! Daddy, you're home!" Since the first one could speak and crawl, I've been welcomed with such tremendous joy. I embrace every day I can experience that moment, an event usually lost as children move into their late adolescence years. Traditionally, I hug, kiss, tackle, chase, or just let them hang from my neck or leg. I drop my briefcase and rush up the stairs to shed myself of my work clothes and change into my Daddy uniform, to hear a million questions and comments about the day that had passed and the night ahead. I used to watch Pamela drift off for 20-30 minutes to recharge her battery as I engaged, embraced, and re-energized my little rug rats, leaving the corporate pressures behind.

Since that dreadful day in February the routine hasn't changed, except she's not there to smile and drift off, and the truth is I've never been able to relieve myself of my work clothes. Today I may act the same; but sometimes it's clear I'm faking my way to the daddy locker room to change clothes, and at times I just don't have it in me to unplug from the real world. The face of that father has never been the same.

Being a Dad was never a job until February 18, 2007, when I was hired with no interview, no offer letter, no compensation discussion, just forced to accept the position of single parent. I miss with such fervor the young man who used to come jetting out of his car in the driveway. Pamela, the mother of my children, is not coming back. I know he's not coming back, either. That loss I can't seem to come to terms with, at least not for today. It hurts, but I push on through because I know—like all loss—it has an end. I just don't know when this face will change to the point I accept its reflection in the mirror.

CHAPTER EIGHTEEN

Fortune 500 Farm Boy

Using his mix of street sense, book smarts, and good old Farm Boy heart,
he put Pamela on the spot—and therefore my entire career.

My first job out of college was with Marriott International, and I worked there for 13 years, learning about corporate America. Every experience taught me not only how to personalize service to meet the expectations of so many different guests, but also what goes on in America's boardrooms. A service industry like the hotel business keeps you humble. Growing into a leader in a hotel company, I quickly realized no matter how high up in the organization you climb, at the end of the day your success still is determined by the basics of being a hotelier, how many toilets you stick your head into, assuring they were cleaned to the highest level of standards for the next guest.

During those first dozen years with Marriott I met many sharp business minds, shaping the man I am today and certainly the leader I've become. We're still so impressionable when in our twenties, maybe even more so than when we're teenagers. I was fortunate to work for the largest employer in the service industry.

I think every organization can outgrow its culture. As Marriott grew into a billion dollar business its fundamentals never changed, but its culture became more challenging to support or witness at every corner. Some of those inconsistencies can be traced back to Marriott's need to change its business model, opening up to franchising in order to grow. I had very little experience with franchising. So, after many years with Marriott, I found myself stuck in a career crossroads. Stay with the big "M" where advancement was behind a crowded political staircase, but in an organization that provided a good living for me and my family? Or take a risk, and take all the knowledge, experience, and training only a big company can offer, and join a smaller hotel company where I'd have a chance at influencing an entire organization vs. just a hotel team?

One day I came home to tell Pamela I was interested in leaving Marriott. She was shocked, but after much discussion we were on the same page. I hadn't selected where I'd go or who I'd work for. It was going to be a careful decision. We had a great life and she reminded me never to put our paychecks before personal happiness. However, she also knew happiness at home comes from enjoying what you do for a living, and who you do it for. After all, it's where we spend most of our adult lives, especially in a business open 24 hours a day, every day of the year, including Christmas.

After spending over a decade with Marriott and having planned to retire with the company that took me in as a college kid, I finally made the decision to leave. I was going to work for Concord Hospitality, the company I'm still with ten years later. When Concord made me an offer, the first step was to sit down at the dinner table with Pamela and lay out all the cards. I had a feeling this was going to go pretty easy, in large part because we were moving to Northern New Jersey. Growing up in the rival sports town, I'd learned to despise Jersey, but Northern Jersey was where Pamela grew up so it was a dream come true for her mom when we moved to a home fifteen minutes from hers. It meant Lyn could play grandma any time it could fit in her day.

I came across Concord through the advice of a previous boss, Dan, who'd become a good friend and mentor. Dan had made the jump to a franchise company just a year earlier and was having great success. When Dan learned I was considering a move from Marriott, he connected me with Bob, Concord's Chief Operating Officer who, like Dan, had left Marriott for bigger responsibilities and a chance to head an entire work force into the future. Bob would hire me to run a few of Concord's hotels in Northern Jersey.

It was definitely a different environment. At the time I left Marriott it was one of the largest service industry companies in the world. Marriott had more than 3,000 hotels worldwide and almost 500,000 employees in almost every corner of the globe. When I made the leap of faith to join Concord they had just reached 30 hotels. At that stage in my career I knew big didn't always mean better, but little did I know I was about to work for one of the best leaders I'd ever encounter.

What made working for Bob such a learning experience was not his experienced background in the industry, or his efficient managerial style as an executive growing a young company. It was the opportunity to learn from a man who'd spent his early years of his life growing up in one of the most important business roles in this country—entrepreneurship. Bob had cut his teeth on the fundamentals of entrepreneurship long before working in the hotel industry. He was a son of a milk farmer. Farming is one of the worlds most important but risky entrepreneurial industries you will find in corporate America today.

Bob carried a nickname from a cartoon made popular in the 90s, "Bob the Builder." I thought it was because he could lay the hammer down on people when needed. I now know, even if it was unintentional, his nickname matched his leadership ability. Bob definitely knew how to build a company and, more specifically, craft a company culture.

Companies have mission statements meant to be a rallying cry, their business pledge of allegiance. At Concord we've documented our Four Cornerstones of Success—otherwise known as our company values. I've learned, however, that the real identity of a company is not the documented mission statement or spoken values. The heartbeat of a company, its soul, is its culture.

Mark Laport, president and founder of Concord, is a great man in his own right. Mark is not just the recognized face of Concord in the industry but the one who took the biggest risk in starting the company. Mark definitely *is* Concord. But back then he entrusted Bob to grow the *soul* of Concord, and when Pamela became very ill with cancer, Bob gave me the leadership lesson of a lifetime. That's when I learned that farmers can make the best CEOs.

I knew being a senior-level executive like Bob meant being able to run with the big boys in the Fortune 500 community. What I didn't realize was you also needed to have the wisdom and ability to rally those who work for you, and enlist their time and engage their unwavering support when one of your own is faced with the painful adversity of dealing with a family tragedy. Bob Micklash—Chief Operating Officer for Concord Hospitality, son of a farmer, and overall respected, successful business leader—did just that.

It's important to know how Bob entered Pamela's life for the first time, before she was diagnosed with leukemia and Bob, Mark and Concord came to our aid. I'd worked for Concord for several years running the Renaissance Meadowlands Hotel. I loved that hotel. I can remember telling Bob it was my dream job and I figured I'd be running it for at least the next five years.

Then a position opened up in our corporate office in Raleigh—Vice President of Sales and Marketing. I had a great desire to speak up about the kind of leader we needed in this critical company role, to support the Concord leaders running our hotels. The short story is that my mouth—I like to think my strategic opinions—caused Bob to ask, "Why not consider the job yourself?" VP of Sales and Marketing for a hotel company that did over 100 million in sales a year? I'd never had a sales-titled position in my life. It sounded crazy to me, but I wasn't Bob. And it didn't sound crazy to Bob. This was one of many learned lessons, working for the Fortune 500 Farm Boy.

I was in shock. Pamela and I had another one of those career dinner table chats, this one lasting two or three meals. First I had to come down from the honor of being asked to consider such a role. Then Pamela and I had to think through the implications of a traveling job, as well as having to move again. Moving itself was not the biggest issue. No, the issue was moving south to Raleigh, a place where neither of us had ever been or had any desire to live. More important, it would take us 8-9 hours from Grandma Lyn who'd been ten minutes away, and from my parents who'd been just over an hour away. Not an easy choice or simple conversation.

In the end, we agreed it was a great opportunity for our family, so I'd throw my name in the hat. The next day I called Bob to tell him we were very interested. I say "we" because Bob had made it clear that in his mind this was not my decision alone. Pamela needed to believe in it as much as I did.

Lesson Number One from a Fortune 500 Farm Boy: As you grow people and give them significant roles in the organization, you have to make sure not only are they committed to the job but—more importantly—the family members they leave each morning are equally supportive and aware of the job's responsibilities.

After some initial interviews, Bob flew Pamela and me to Raleigh. He wanted us to get a feel for where we'd live and the schools that would help raise our kids. I'd never been flown to a city before to "just check it out and look around" before I even had a position. I remember feeling like some big time, professional sports star, having owners wine and dine us so I'd play for their city. Actually, Bob did wine and dine us. He invited us to dinner with him and his wife, Karen, and Mark and his wife Vicki.

Here were the wives of the president and founder of Concord and the COO, neither of whom Pamela had met. I'd met Mark Laport many times, but never had I been at a dinner table with him and certainly not as the center of attention and purpose for the occasion. The invitation was beginning to move from exciting to overwhelming and quickly to stressful. I never let on to Pamela that I was getting worked up about the dinner. I knew if she was relaxed and simply herself, they'd all love her.

We went to a fancy steakhouse and everyone was getting along so well it was almost like family. I could see Bob and Mark really took to Pamela, and their wives seemed to genuinely enjoy meeting her and, I think, me as well. Then, after our first glass of wine and some appetizers, the socializing experience of a lifetime came to a screeching halt. In Bob-the-Builder-like fashion, using his mix of street sense, book smarts, and good old Farm Boy heart, he put Pamela on the spot—and therefore my entire career. "Pamela, how are you going to be able to handle Kevin being in this new role, in a position that requires travel, and now based in Raleigh, North Carolina?" He didn't spare any punches, going on to say, "I know your mom lived around the corner in New Jersey, and with three little kids at home, that's going to be tough, not having family living nearby to help you." He topped it off with, "Are you sure this is what's best for the two of you?"

Before Pamela answered I thought to myself, *Is he out of his damn mind? What the hell is this? Who flies a couple five states from home, takes them out to a fancy dinner with the president of the company, which appeared to be a social event to ensure we all got along, to now find out it was a set-up to pose a career suicide question to my wife?* And then the voice in my head really panicked, *Oh crap, how is she going to answer this?* What I wanted to say was "Damn it, Bob, she's been a stay-at-home mom for more than four years, not practicing interview skills with men who live in the corner office on the executive floor!" I couldn't even look at Pamela.

She put her fork down and dove right into the question. "Well, Bob and Mark, maybe you don't understand what it's like for us today, but Kevin works very hard for Concord and his hotel. There are many nights during the week when he may not get home until 8 o'clock. He does, of course, make sure he's home several nights a week in time to help me."

She went on, "Understand, I get the reality of the hours he needs to work. I worked retail for more than ten years, which is almost always late nights and weekend shifts. I understand what it takes for Kevin to be successful, and we make it work. When he's home, he is totally *on* as a dad. He also works at the hotel every weekend. Frankly, the kids and I miss not having him at home, but if you put him in this position, my guess is he won't get calls at ten o'clock at night telling him there's an emergency at work and he has to get to the hotel immediately. If he has to get some work completed on weekends it can be done in the living room, not 45 minutes away from me and the kids. I know he'll have to travel, and many nights I'll have to feed, bath, and tuck in our three kids, but I think you can see that's no different than it is today."

She wrapped it up with, "Actually this job would bring a better balance to our lives as parents. Can you see what I mean?"

I thought *Holy Cow, that ball is out-of-here, homerun! It was amazing, thank goodness we didn't rehearse that question because I would have totally screwed it up. She just smacked a hard ball right back at the COO and at the same time gave me a high recommendation to the president, not to mention probably making two wives sitting at the table fall in love with her as a mother, a wife, and a woman.*

Needless to say, after dinner we enjoyed several adult cocktails, then we flew home and packed our bags for Raleigh.

As a farmer I imagine one loves and cares for your animals and the very ground you live on, and Bob cared for us and our families in the same way. To him we were his flock. He was there to cultivate careers and make dreams come true, not just for those who worked for Concord, but for their families. In three short years he had now offered me my second dream job.

I wish I could say, "Let's fast forward a few years to when we first knew Pamela was sick." Unfortunately, it was only a couple of months after the move to Raleigh that Pamela was diagnosed with leukemia.

There are many vivid memories, or should I say nightmares, of those first few days when our lives changed forever. Finding out she had cancer was a complete shock to us. As a matter of fact, it was diagnosed from a visit to the walk-in clinic because she was feeling fatigued, a normal symptom of motherhood with three little kids and having recently unpacked an entire house. Her blood work was suspicious to the clinic staff and she had an appointment later that day with a specialist. I remember her calling me at work, saying the doctor at the clinic suggested her husband come to the appointment, which of course made her feel nervous. The physician at the clinic wouldn't say what was wrong, just that it would take a specialist to nail it down exactly.

What really scared her, though, was when the nurse held the door open for her as she exited the clinic. She was pushing Christopher in the stroller and holding Amanda's hand on the way out when the nurse said, "I'll say a prayer for you." A prayer? Earlier that morning when we discussed Pamela going to get checked out we didn't think it was anything more than some kind of vitamin deficiency, something a change of diet or some meds would correct. How little we knew. The nurse was not tossing out prayers to everyone at the clinic. She knew enough about what the blood work showed to know Pamela was about to be in the battle of her life—for her life.

Pamela was told later that afternoon she needed to get to Rex Hospital that night and be in the care of the cancer center as soon as possible. We went home, made lots of calls to family, shedding tears in the absence of the kids' little ears, and figured out what we'd tell the kids so they weren't frightened when Mommy wasn't home that night. As days went by and our family, friends and co-workers became aware of Pamela's diagnosis, many wanted to come see her. Pamela was not in the mood for visitors. Both of us were exhausted from stress and depression, and I from racing back and forth between daddy duties and being by her bedside for husband duty. Pamela was fatigued from chemo, which started the day after she checked-in, and asked that I not let anyone visit her. We did understand how hard it was for all those who cared about us, worried about her, and wanted to do something to help show support. In most cases we said, "If you want to help—bring dinner or do something fun with the kids to keep their minds off missing Pamela." We wouldn't know what kind of help or support we needed until we could figure out what kind of mess we were in.

Well the Farm Boy from Michigan wouldn't have it. One afternoon when we were in the hospital, he called and said he and Karen were in the area and they wanted to see Pamela. He easily convinced me that a visit from him showing Concord's support would be a good thing for her. I'd seen the effects of the chemo and missing the kids in her demeanor that morning, and knew it was time to do what I thought was best for her emotionally, and not take all her requests as law. Bob wanted to make sure Pamela knew, from the president of the company, that she and I needed to be in the business of only one thing, "Getting her well," and she was not to be concerned about my position with Concord or any lost time at work. I have to admit I never questioned it myself, but I knew seeing Bob would ease my mind as well.

He promised his visit would take no more than a few minutes. I didn't tell Pamela he was coming, and hovered in and out of her hospital room door so I could make sure he didn't get held back by the nursing staff when he arrived. When Bob and Karen turned the hallway corner, for the first time in my life I broke down and cried in front of a co-worker, and this one was my boss. It certainly was not the reaction I expected from myself, but as they drew near I could see the pain he felt for us reflected in his eyes—as if he were staring right into my heart. Using every muscle in my body, I tried to keep my composure: "She can't die, she has to be all right. I don't know how I will make it without her."

Bob supported us in so many ingenious ways while Pamela battled her illness and also when the kids and I had to face the hard reality of our life without Mommy. A corporate peer and mutual close friend, Pam, and I often wondered at the source of Bob's wisdom and ability to move so swiftly yet responsibly to help, knowing when to handle something, when to just show love and care, and how to engage everyone or flip a switch to back people off when we needed to work through our pain and despair. All of this was the equivalent of a master's degree in human science that even professional therapists would struggle to orchestrate.

I know there's no textbook out there for CEOs on how to handle desperate family situations, but if there were, it would have a chapter in it called the Concord Cultural Care Checklist. Think of all the attention Bob paid to me and my family, while he had millions in profits to manage, thousands of employees taking care of guests each day in numerous cities across the U.S. and Canada. Yet he got up early, tended to the cows one at a time, and taught an organization how to have soul.

Bob left Concord a few years later for an opportunity to go from running 50 hotels to more than 800 hotels. That's a big flock to tend to. When he left, so did a piece of Concord's soul. But he left behind a heartbeat of what he brought to this great company—me and many others who were touched by this Farm Boy from Michigan.

I remember one of my first meetings with Nick, our new Chief Operating Officer, who replaced Bob. It was an uneasy time, having Bob leave after he'd done so much to raise my career in this industry, also at the time the country was in the deepest part of the recession. Due to Nick being new to our team, and his awareness that many of us were uneasy witnessing layoffs outside the organization with our peer competitors, he held rap sessions with each of us in his first few weeks. I remember him asking, "So how do you feel about your job? Are you happy with what you're doing and Concord, or do you have thoughts of leaving us?"

At first I thought to myself, *Uh oh, I didn't have thoughts of leaving until you just asked me.* Instead I answered him from the heart: "Nick, I don't know how much of my situation you're aware of, but I'll give it to you straight. The only way I am ever leaving this company is if you tell me to. I have blind, unshakable loyalty to Concord, and Mark Laport, for all this company did to help pull me and my kids out of the worst event in our lives. Bob surely was at the heart of a lot of what went on, but Mark never once stopped him or asked him to slow down the support the company was offering me. Therefore you can stop paying me, or treat me like crap, and I'm still showing up because I owe that to Concord."

Nick in his dry British humor way replied, "Ah, good, so you're happy with your role. Excellent."

I wonder where I'd be in my life or in my career had Pamela choked and answered that question at dinner differently. No sense pondering it, because she didn't. She knocked it out of the park, as did Bob Micklash every day he came through the doors of Concord.

....

CHAPTER NINETEEN

Have the Courage to Ride the Waves

"Can there possibly be such a thing as a last tear?"

As a child, my favorite place in the whole world was the Wildwood, New Jersey coast, otherwise known as the Jersey shore. Every summer my parents, my brother, and I spent two weeks in a rental house just a few blocks from the long, white, sandy beach at Wildwood. Dozens of cousins, uncles, aunts, and my grandparents would rent houses nearby so we could all gather on the beach each day, embracing one of the great McAteer family traditions.

Something about the shore touches the soul. Those boyhood memories of Thanksgiving-like gatherings of family made me appreciate every beach I'd visit along the coast of the Atlantic Ocean. As I grew into my teenage years, I gained a greater appreciation for the serenity of one of nature's miracles. To walk along the sand and feel the calm morning tide pour over your footprints in the sand, then in the evening hearing the powerful roar of the waves putting you to sleep at night, all makes the shore the closest place to heaven in my mind.

I never imagined the beach and the ocean's push and pull as an analogy of life, until I lost Pamela to cancer.

I remember anxiously anticipating a therapy session with Terry, the counselor at Rex Hospital. Normally, I'd spend a lot of energy in the hours before our time together, reflecting on how I was feeling and where I was in the process of grieving. It was an easy prediction that Terry's first question would be, "So how is Kevin doing today?" I wanted our time to be productive because I had so little of it with all that was going on with the children, the home and my job. Every minute was so valuable I knew I couldn't afford *not* to make those meetings as introspective and honest as possible, so I could take some baby steps forward. Well aware, I should expect to take big leaps backwards each week. I really missed having Pamela in my life so much.

Before this particular meeting I was daydreaming about the shore, realizing how waking up each morning and taking on our momentous loss was like walking out into that ocean in my youth and feeling the waves' rugged approach to us *wannabe beach bums.*

Why the comparison of such a wonderful time in my life with the most devastating? Was it because I asked Pamela to marry me many years earlier on that very beach in Wildwood, New Jersey? Or because, months after our traditional church wedding, we held a second wedding celebration at the beach in Bayhead, New Jersey—in front of her father's beach house where she had a photo album full of childhood memories? Maybe, but more true was the parallel of walking on the beach to the water, waking up each day guessing how the waves would hit you unexpectedly.

Learning how to body surf, to ride those waves from deep in the ocean all the way onto the beach front, is one of the most thrilling discoveries a kid can ever experience. Christopher reminded me of that when we spent a weekend at the beach along the coast of North Carolina.

I second guessed getting up the morning of February 18, 2007, like that first time a child second guesses if they should walk deeper into the ocean or just stay back on the sand. Once a young child has conquered their fear of the ocean, it's easy to run across that beach and into God's great waters. However, they learn the waves roll into the shore in many unpredictable ways:

- The first time I watched Christopher's little body get out there I wondered will a wave roar in, seemingly ready to devour him, but then seconds before closing in on him, just fizzles out and becomes nothing but a weak brush against the skin?
- Would he be caught off guard with a wave that seems to be easy to manage but, as it grows near, picks up sudden power and knocks him off his feet and forces him to quickly gather his balance to be ready in case another comes racing behind the first blow?
- Or does this little boy walk out into the ocean, surprised to find it's as calm as a pond in the early morning, with not even a ripple in front of him?

Christopher had not learned yet there also can be waves with God's aggressiveness behind them. We feel we can brace ourselves in advance, but they not only knock us off our feet, they take us to our knees, bend our backs with such pain and weakness in our muscles, we want to wish the moment away—wondering if we'll get our heads above water and breathe in time to make it back to the beach.

After Pamela died, I honestly never knew how each moment and each day would go. On days like her birthday, I'd prepare for the worst storm, only to find the waves didn't pack much of a punch. Then, in a normal everyday walk up our driveway to the mailbox, from what seemed to be calm waters, a wave would suddenly bring me to my knees in a moment of deep loss and pain.

My friend Matt, who'd lost his daughter many years earlier, told me about driving his motorcycle to work on what would have been her 9th birthday. He knew there might be some waves but he wanted that date for once to feel normal, at least during the work shift. As he made it to the traffic light one block from our office, he came to a red light and suddenly found himself fogging up his motorcycle mask with tears. He thought, *Aw, come on man, not now, just let me get to work, not while I'm driving the bike. I don't want to grieve right now.* But there was nothing he could do. He had to pull over and let the wave take its course. Once he found the strength to get back up and rub the pain from his eyes, he got on his bike, drove to work, and actually made it through the entire day without another wave pinning him to the ocean floor.

Why did Matt's day unwind that way? I believe it's because those big days are like stepping out into the ocean and bracing yourself. I spent the whole day on the second anniversary of Pamela's death waiting for the debilitation, but it never came. Then days later—on a normal, mundane Thursday—my daughter out of nowhere said, "Daddy, I miss Mommy." I rushed to another room, and sobbed uncontrollably, wondering, *Can there possibly be such a thing as a last tear?*

When I walked into my meeting with Terry that day, as expected she asked her predictable opening question: "How is Kevin today?"

"I'm okay, Terry," I said. "Every day is like waking up at the shore and heading to the beach like when I was growing up. You get up each morning and step out into the ocean of life, knowing you can't predict when the waves will come or what they'll be like. But it's your life, so you have to go from the sand into the water. I may not know when the wave is coming or what kind it will be, but I do know it will eventually pass. The important thing for the kids and for me is that I get up each morning and have the courage to walk out into the ocean, because of that I can say today, 'I'm okay.'"

CHAPTER TWENTY

The Poor Pizza Man

When he left our house that night, Tommy was no longer just a pizza devliery boy.

When you think of professions that people enter knowing it's going to be a pressure cooker, you think of a fireman, President of the United States, or maybe a brain surgeon. Somewhere way down at the bottom of the list you don't see Pizza Delivery Man. Sure, there's some level of pressure in any customer service position. I guess Domino's didn't help when years ago they came out with the "30 minutes or it's free" guarantee. Regardless, when young Tommy—who had to be no more than 17 years old—asked his parents if he could apply for a job as the delivery man for our local Raleigh Papa Johns, I'm sure they thought, "Well there's a decent paying job with an age-appropriate level of responsibility, having to drive pies around the neighborhood. That shouldn't cause our boy any undue stress."

Oh, how wrong they were on this calm Friday night in mid-March. I don't recall the exact date, but I'm guessing for Tommy, the probably newly licensed teenager with the glowing Papa John's sign lighting the rooftop of his parents' Mazda, it was as horrifying as Friday the 13th.

Within weeks after we were on our own, the kids and I had started a tradition. During the week I ran a Parent Decathlon featuring routine events such as staying on top of the kids' homework, trying to feed them something healthier than chicken nuggets, racing them to school in the morning, trying not to forget to get them from after-school activities, and the final laps of tubs, teeth brushing, and tuck-ins.

When Friday night came, all caution was thrown to the wind. Friday nights became FAMILY GAME NIGHT. Three things were always a staple on Family Game Night:

1. The Pizza Man always cooked dinner and delivered it.
2. For at least one hour the four of us tried to play a game together and giggle at the sweat that poured off Daddy's temples as he tried to organize and enjoy a board game or card game with three kids at three different age development levels.
3. Due to #2, Daddy always came to the game table with a Blockbuster movie as back-up.

This particular Friday night I came home hungry and the kids came home from school wound up. I quickly called the pizza man and got our Pizza & Wing order, in preparation for the long sixty minutes of gaming in front of me. A food break was going to be key for me to not go nuts every time I heard my six-year-old yell at Christopher, who was not even three years old at the time, "Noooooo, Chris—tooo—ferrrr. It's not your turn! Uggghhhh, Dadddyyyyyyyy."

That nice cheer was always followed by a request to re-teach Christopher the game rules. That request was always followed by my response, "Yeah, I'll get right on that. Who's next?"

Finally, after an eternity, the Heineken started to kick in and I'd lost my VP of Sales hat long enough to relax among the chaos of a game of Candyland. Then, just as the good times were rolling, the doorbell rang, followed by all three kids yelling in unison, "Pizza Man is here!" Ahh, my night was getting better. Unfortunately, Tommy's was about to head south, in a hurry.

After the collective cheer, "The Pizza Man is here, he's here, he's here" next came a mad dash to the door by my three energetic, yet immature roommates to see who could be the first one to greet this unsuspecting messiah with the big square box in his hand.

Our house can be a bit confusing to the delivery guys as there are two front entrances and strangers don't know which is the common one. Kevin Patrick ran to the door we normally use by the kitchen. Amanda, as usual, followed several slow steps behind her idol, her big brother. C.J. the always predictable non-conformer, headed to the opposite door by the dining room.

Normally I get hijacked for the money so one kid can own the proud honor of being the one to say "I paid the pizza man." However, since I'd rushed to get our order in this night, I hadn't laid out the pizza man money and had to grab my wallet.

Christopher and all of his 25 pounds of exuberant energy beat his older siblings and picked the right door. With eyes wide open, full of pride, he reached high up, attempting to jiggle the front door handle open. I was fumbling through my wallet to get the money, getting a glimpse of Tommy as he tentatively reached to help C.J. open the door without dropping our food. I was trying to rush so I could get to the door, for Tommy's sake, to avoid his being left alone with the exuberant C.J. They looked really cute as I approached the door from a side angle, out of C.J. and Pizza Boy's view. Tommy had a boyish smile on his face, almost like an older cousin full of fondness for his young buddy. You could see he was enjoying the dialogue with my miniature doorman. Christopher in his unpredictable sweetness, kept chatting it up with this total stranger that he'd instantly bonded with at the threshold of our front door.

"Is that your car?"

"Ah, you mean the one with the pizza sign on the roof? Ah yeah."

I stopped to soak in the heart-warming exchange of the two boys but went to Tommy's rescue when I saw he'd run out of small talk for the little guy. Then, before I could make my presence known to both of them, it happened. Tommy asked his newfound friend a simple question: "Um… is your mommy home?"

Christopher responded, "My mommy died," his big brown eyes gazing innocently at his new idol.

Tommy was stunned. I could tell he knew this boy was not lying. But life had not yet prepared him to deal with that answer, and so he had no reply.

I tried to get to the door to stop Tommy from having to counter Christopher's response, but I could not save him. On that night Tommy arrived a teenage boy making his parents proud by taking on the responsibility of a pizza delivery job. When he left our house that night, Tommy was no longer just a pizza delivery boy. He had handled his responsibilities as a man. I couldn't get Tommy out of my mind, wondering what his response might be to his mom when he came home after his shift was over and she asked, "How was work, Son?"

....

CHAPTER TWENTY-ONE

Time to Empty it Out, Take it Down, and Change it Around

Honor was laid out on the battlefield of single parenting every day.
I didn't need to represent it by not reorganizing her dresser.

Although my hours were totally invested in the kids' needs and emotions for months after Pamela left us, every once in a while—late at night or early in the morning—a moment to myself would appear. If I wasn't treading water from a tidal wave of grief, I'd normally take mental inventory. What was the next logical change I was expected to manage now that I was alone? I realized one night how much Pamela and I loved cataloguing all the kids' moments in photos. As I strolled the house after being blessed with an early bedtime for all three, it startled me to see how many framed pictures were in every room. Not only that, I was dumbfounded to find the same picture in three different rooms in the house, all in different frames, each its unique size. That night I also realized I hadn't made one change to any of Pamela's stuff; everything was in the exact same place it was on February 17th. My life had turned 360 degrees, but everything inside this place we call home was exactly the same.

I thought about stories I'd heard or maybe it was the thousand Lifetime movies I'd seen (one of Pamela's favorite TV channels, which I'd only watch for a few minutes—I swear!) where a family might not change a bedroom to honor a lost loved one and keep her memory alive. That seemed logical, but it just didn't fit inside my skin and definitely was not an aid to my grieving process. Pamela's memory was alive and well. As a matter of fact, her memory woke me each morning before 6 am in the shape of a three-year-old boy or a set of four-year-old, blond ponytails. Honor was laid out on the battlefield of single parenting every day. I didn't need to represent it by not reorganizing her dresser. Honor was something that kicked in at 11 pm, when I'd do all I could to make sure the house was picked up. I would wander the place picking up Hot Wheels and crayons, putting away bikes and balls under the moonlight in the driveway. Those were the things Pamela somehow accomplished while caring for three little ones each day. Before I passed out each night I was honoring her by trying to mimic what she had done every day for the four of us.

My career and work ethic may have given us the financial wellbeing to afford a nice place to live, but Pamela's work ethic and successful career as a stay-at-home mom made this place an amazing HOME to live in. I was committed to doing my best to not let it slip into a fraternity house of chicken nuggets for breakfast, and every dinner served up with ketchup.

However, for me it was time to make changes. Everything had changed, so why not the walls and the dressers? Heck, Pamela would change furniture around daily; I would take my dress shirt out of a cabinet before work and then come home to find it had changed to an underwear drawer. Maybe in a way I was honoring her traits as a homemaker. So I made changes with no regard to anyone else's opinion as to whether it was "time." If it was time for me, and if it didn't have a negative impact on the kids, then guess what? It was time.

Nightly I would go through her clothes and clear off the shelves, replacing them with my own; I boxed some of her stuff for the kids to give them later in life. Other items I would place in the kids' rooms. Even though her t-shirts were too large, I knew certain ones represented who she was to each of them. They quickly picked up the habit of wearing one of Mommy's shirts to bed as pajamas every few days. It was cute, but brought on some tears. I also mailed things to her closest loved ones to let them have a concrete piece of her to remember. It might be a pair of costume jewelry earrings that for sure were "Pamela." It might be a few sweatshirts or t-shirts that I knew would spur on some fun memories for others.

Other nights I would take down pictures, always putting up new ones, but this time no duplicates. One night, in a moment of hatred toward cancer, I took down every picture in the house that just showed Pamela and me and replaced them with pictures of the five of us. Cancer ended my marriage, and for me at that time it was frankly stupid to remind myself of a marriage between two people before the kids were born. I was no longer married! But we were still a family and Pamela was still their mother.

I was confronted with one of the most difficult changes to make on a night I was not even at home. After work I had a dinner to attend and a babysitter was watching the kids. I made a call home to say goodnight and I guess the kids were engrossed in a movie and the babysitter didn't feel comfortable answering our home phone. The phone rang three times and went to voicemail. For the first time in months, I heard Pamela's voice and it stung with such intensity! I was totally not prepared to hear her voice, especially sounding so joyful. This time I couldn't crack a smile through the tears. The following weekend I finally found the right moment to change the message, so others wouldn't go through what I had experienced. I wrote a funny script and found the right voiceover, Amanda! Her tiny, sweet voice with its high pitched tone was perfect, and she was the only person who could have made it feel OK to erase a memory forever. It was not easy knowing I'd heard Pamela's voice for the last time when I called home.

Years later I heard and read so much advice for grieving parents and husbands/wives on how to handle the difficulties of "having" to address taking the pictures down, or emptying the closets of a lost loved one. Opinions of those on the outside never seemed that supportive or understanding. I'd hear "He/she is hanging on too much; it's not healthy to not have changed the bedroom a year later," or, "That guy is a real piece of work. Do you know he sold her car already?" and, "He's dating. I knew he didn't love her as much as everyone thought."

There are times when we don't have the privilege of handling change on our own terms, like when a grandparent passes away and an apartment has to be emptied out because it's been rented by a new tenant. Hopefully most of us won't *have* to address anything, except making sure you're doing what feels healthy for you and surrounding yourself with grief counselors who understand that dealing with your loss is not like anyone else's. Every life is unique and special; therefore, every loss of life and how we get through it is equally not common with another's situation. Advice from friends and family members is a good thing only when it's led with love and the respect of letting you make your own decisions when it's the right time for you. Offer to help out of sincere caring for the person hurting, but they decide what kind of change they're ready for and when. Should a person start dating a few months or a few years after they've lost their partner? The answer is simple. How the hell would you know? It's not for you to know, and therefore not for you to answer. Love and support come from listening, and feeling the loss with them, being there when others are too busy, and reminding them your love is constant. It's the kind of present they don't need a gift receipt for, because you're not interested in their returning it.

CHAPTER TWENTY-TWO

Where Do I Put My Damn Keys?

On Tuesday the bench would be missing. On Wednesday the shelf would be missing. Every day I came home, furniture I'd swear was brown when I left, was now red.

Pamela was always on the move. She did so much you'd expect to hear people say, "Wow, that woman has an incredible work ethic." It's interesting, however, that in all the years I knew Pamela I never heard anyone refer to her as "such a hard worker." I think the main reason is that she made everything look so easy with a friendly personality and warm spirit, what she was doing didn't seem like "work" to her, but rather just living in the moment.

When the roster at home began to include three children, Pamela stopped working in her field of retailing. We both wanted her to spend every moment she could raising the children, since running hotels meant I might need to work all kinds of different hours each week. Once she stopped working at the local clothing store, her days became much more exhausting chasing the three children around and keeping up a beautiful home.

We took great pride in choosing the homes we raised our family in, and each of us played a unique role in becoming responsible home owners. Pamela would pick out the house she'd love us to live in; I'd make the final decision on whether we could afford it, knowing there was always a chance we'd have to move because of my career. Selling our home was almost as important as buying it.

Pamela was in charge of decorating each house, which meant she made it "home". She had a great eye for making any room look so much more inviting after adding her touch. All I ever asked was to have one room to call my own, which meant it would be covered in pictures and memorabilia of all the Philadelphia sports teams.

We even had the perfect recipe for managing money in a marriage. I earned most of our money, and paid the bills. She earned most of the moments with the kids, and did the spending. Thankfully, Pamela always found the best deals and made every dollar go further than the stingiest accountant.

We were the perfect fit as cooperative home owners, except for one problem. I never knew where to put my damn keys when I arrived home from work.

I know you're thinking that doesn't seem like much of a marital problem. However, the issue was much bigger than just finding a place to toss my keys and wallet. You see, Pamela loved decorating our home so much and possessed such a feverish work ethic, she never stopped "redecorating." I could come home on a Monday, set my keys on a bench right inside the doorway; then on Tuesday the bench would be missing and I'd find it stationed in another room, so I'd then choose a small basket on a shelf near the doorway to keep my keys safe. On Wednesday the shelf would be missing, replaced by a tall lamp and picture hanging on the wall. It was crazy. Every day I came home I could find an entire room completely reorganized, or maybe furniture I'd swear was brown when I left for work now looked as if it had been recently repainted red.

I didn't know if I should be excited that the home I loved seemed to change every day, or be concerned that I was losing my memory. I could never quite remember where things were. I know people misplace their watch or sunglasses from time to time, but they don't forget the location of a lamp or dresser. The truth is, rather than get excited or concerned; I just sat back in awe. How does a mother with one infant and two toddlers who gets up through the middle of the night to feed at least one of them, then get all this hard labor done with nothing more than a smile on her face, a twinkle in her eye, and of course some Sherman Williams paint, on her fingertips and on the tail of the dog?

The classic defining moment would be when I'd come home after a long, tiring day at work, open the door, and be greeted with the heartwarming sound of little feet running from the other room screaming, "Daddy's home, Daddy's home." As I set my keys down to free both my arms to grab those little angels of energy, you would hear CRASH, as my keys would hit the floor. Once again, the familiar layout of the room had changed. With many emotions running through my veins I would let out a giant scream that would echo through the house:

"Pamela, where the hell am I supposed to keep my keyssssssss?"

CHAPTER TWENTY-THREE

It's Not Just About Making the Bed

"You're making the bed? I AM STILL IN IT.
You can't just make a bed with someone still in it."

Making your bed in the morning can be a real drag. But some people can't get going in the morning unless the bed they slept in is in order. I've discovered over the past fifteen years that making the bed is not about finishing a chore, or a cause for parents to argue with their children. No, it's so much more. For many in this world, making the bed creates an internal sense of place. It's a reflection of one's character and being.

One morning I walked into my second-grade daughter's room. What caught me by surprise was not that—once again—she'd left her lights on as she ran to the bus stop, but that her bed was so perfectly made. I suddenly understood that for Amanda making her bed was about pride, honor, and character that I believe has been passed down in her genes from her mom.

When Pamela was younger she never, *ever* kept her room neat. Lyn used to take joy in telling stories of how Pamela's closet seemed to spread like volcanic lava. Dresses, shoes, shirts, socks, shoes, pants, shoes were always thrown about her entire room. Oh, and did I mention shoes? It was funny to hear those stories because since I'd known Pamela, her room had always been in order.

Now that I look back, Lyn was telling a story about raising a daughter, a story of learning. Similar to when moms teach little girls how to style their hair, do crafts, or paint each other's nails. These were stories of growing up from a baby, to a little girl, and then to a young woman.

As a man, I compare it to hearing stories of sons learning to drive for the first time with their dads, or maybe an old ball coach cracking jokes about how uncoordinated his star athlete was when he first coached him as a youngster.

When Lyn told this story, Pamela would smirk from ear to ear, with a gleam in her eyes. It was an embarrassing story, but also one of pride and honor—pride in gaining the respect of her mom, honor because it was a task they fought about on the battlefield of parenting for most of her youth. I think it was a chance for Lyn to show she was right but also how, as a mother, she paid the price of continually driving home the value of responsibility and care of one's room and, therefore, caring for oneself. I could feel Pamela's sense of honor towards her mom—reflecting who Pamela had become as a woman and her respect and love for the woman who raised her. Who knows, it could have been an emotional connection all the way back to her grandmother.

I have to say, though, making the bed is not always a sign of respect. During our marriage I would almost suggest it was a sign of disrespect. You see, Pamela was so fixated on getting that bed made in the morning, many times when she woke up she'd start making the bed while I was still in it, and, oh yes, sleeping! I've never been known as a guy who sleeps in, except maybe on Father's Day. But once in a while I would work long and late hours at the hotel, so sleeping 30-45 minutes later was more a need to keep my battery charged for the day ahead.

I vividly recall feeling the bedspread tugging away from me one morning, as if the person next to me was rolling over and I'd soon be left with no sheets unless I took my position in the tug of war. I didn't want to wake her, or myself for that matter, so I gently untucked some of the sheets from the bottom of the bed and secured them under my feet. I could hear some rustling but not enough for me to bother opening an eye. Then the sheets under my feet were pulled out. Man, I was getting annoyed. But I didn't know if it was maybe one of the kids. I slowly opened my eyes, not moving another muscle in case I needed to fall into "fake daddy sleep coma." As I peeked up, I could see it was Pamela and she was up and ready for the day. I raised my head and looked around. To my surprise, her entire side of the bed was perfectly made. Then I watched as she began to smooth the sheets and tuck them into the bottom of the bed, including where my tired feet were. I asked the obvious question. "What are you doing?"

She said, "Oh. I'm making the bed."

"What! You're making the bed? I AM STILL IN IT. You can't just make a bed with someone still in it. WHO DOES THAT?"

Pamela, in her kind, gentle way, said, "Oh sorry. Didn't mean to wake you; go back to sleep."

I have only one word for that whole incident. "REALLY?"

This may all seem a bit silly, or maybe a little over-thought. Normally I might agree, but as I mentioned, a few weeks ago I realized it's not just about making the bed.

Amanda was only four years old when Pamela was deep into her illness, and only a few months past her fifth birthday when her mother passed away. It seems odd to me that a little girl so young, and without her number one female role model in life, would learn and perfect such a chore. I mean, let's face it, although it might be a mundane task to adults, we all watch kids struggle to get sheets on a bed or a comforter to fall across to the other side. I swear my boys could work on making their bed for hours and you'd look at the bed and not see a single sign of effort. I think it would look neater if they closed their eyes and tossed their pillows and blankets onto the bed from across the room.

You have to understand, as well, Amanda has not just made her bed for the last several years each morning. She has made her bed every day before ever leaving her bedroom for breakfast or a little morning TV. I mean even the neatest kid has to get a little Nickelodeon or a pop tart in before taking on such a daunting task.

In addition, not only does she make the bed, she makes it in a way that any grandmother, nun, or marine drill sergeant would be proud. Her bed is perfect each morning, every day, before she leaves her room: pillows placed the way a five-star hotel would prepare for the First Lady, sheets and blankets tight over her mattress as if she'd ironed them all morning, running back and forth over the bed. Amanda's desire to make her bed this way has to be something larger, a sense of honor or pride in becoming a woman.

Pondering this brings a smile to my face, but then a sharp pain in my gut. In that moment of realization, I saw a little girl who loved her mommy so much and misses her so much, she probably can't articulate it. I see a little girl who lost some of her childhood to cancer and was forced into being a little woman at the ridiculous age of five years old.

As much as it drives me crazy to bicker over and over with Kevin and Christopher about cleaning up their rooms and making their beds, I sometimes wish I needed to send Amanda back to her room to finally make her bed right. Unfortunately I don't. But I'm proud of her for becoming such a kind, caring, respectful little girl with so many of her mother's qualities, though only getting to be with her mommy up until kindergarten.

I never made my bed growing up. As a matter of fact, I can still hear myself telling my mom and dad, "That's why rooms have doors on them. If it bothers you, shut my door." You'll probably find it hard to believe I've run hotels for a career, and some of the most award-winning hotels for cleanliness and service. When I say I never made my bed growing up, I mean even as a grown up. Not in high school, not in college, not when I went out in the work force and lived on my own, or when I had roommates. I never even made the bed when Pamela and I first lived together. Of course, she would always handle that for me.

It's not just about making the bed.

Why? Because at 43 now I make my bed, too! Is it in honor of Pamela or is it with pride for Amanda? I don't know for sure. I only know I have to do it now—it's a part of who I am when I look inside at my reflection and judge my own character.

CHAPTER TWENTY-FOUR

Real Clowns Dress in Coco Chanel

"It is better to have loved and lost than never to have loved at all."

Wikipedia Definition of Clowns: *Comic performers stereotypically characterized by colored wigs, stylistic makeup, outlandish costumes, unusually large footwear, and red noses, worn to project their actions to large audiences.*

Some clowns you meet can juggle, some can pull a rabbit out of a hat, while others walk around in oversized, floppy shoes. Not my clown. My clown was unique because she always dressed in Chanel. Maybe that's why I fell in love with her over ten years ago.

The first time I met my clown she was wearing a black suit that looked like it came off the rack at Nordstrom, and she walked across the room in black, high-heeled shoes, not floppy sneakers. Instead of a big, red curly wig, her white-blond hair was tightly pulled back in a ponytail with a matching black bow. Although, like most clowns, she loved to wear make-up, her make-up looked like it was barely applied, to bring out her natural beauty. No big wig, no silly clown nose. The only thing fake on her outfit (I later found out) were her earrings. They featured two CC's—which I now know are a trademark for designer Coco Chanel.

My clown was Pamela Jenks. I met her for the first time in her retail clothing store while she was working the sales floor. Our encounter was a fortunate incident of fate, unplanned and unexpected, much like finding out about her career as an actual clown.

This story is about a fashionable, elegant, stunningly attractive beauty who could turn heads from across a room simply by entering it. Although she did attend clown school and performed at one birthday party, her best work was not on stage or under the circus big top. No, her best magical tricks were performed later, almost 15 years after her short stint in clown school. The local park playgrounds, family rooms, or even a basement turned playroom were her stage.

I do call Pamela a clown, but not in the same way I've been nicknamed a clown. Not for pulling practical jokes or trying to be the funny guy at the party. No, Pamela was a clown in the traditional sense, how kids think of them—dreamy, and with a feeling of wonderment. She was pure, endless energy with a constant desire to entertain the children. She lived, heart and soul, to bring joy and comfort to the little ones.

Not all of Pamela's performances are as legendary or as creative as the indoor basement pool. As a matter of fact, the most common story I hear is how several moms would get together late on a Friday afternoon for a mommy happy hour. While most of the women would watch their kids out of the corners of their eyes, you'd always find my clown on the living room floor, playing with the children.

I learned so much from Pamela about how not to lose sight of why we all get so excited the day our children are born. She taught me how easy it is to sit on your bed almost every night, reading to not one, not two, but three kids. I learned that finger painting doesn't have to have a set-up or clean-up plan before you start smothering your kids in blue ink. Still a staple in my house is her lesson that a kitchen table is supposed to be covered in old stains from craft projects.

The most famous of all Pamela's productions would be her last performance for me, captured on film and burned in my mind forever. At that show, my clown did wear a wig on stage, not from her clown trunk hidden in the closet, but from the cancer support wig store reluctantly worn to hide the effects of chemotherapy. The day before she would enter Rex Hospital for the last time, I watched her running around the front yard playing Wiffle Ball with all three of the kids, the four of them laughing and cheering with excitement. She was worn down by the meds she was on, self-conscious of the hair loss she had to live with, but only a clown would put on her make-up, get her wig, and go out to perform for the children.

So, yes, real clowns do wear make-up to hide their identity, but one clown wore it to look like she belonged on the cover of Glamour magazine.

Clowns do make juggling look easy, and one clown amazed us, juggling three kids and a stroller with the heartfelt smile and energy of a tri-athlete.

Clowns can make us warm and happy. When performing they seem to really love life. My clown, too, was ready to perform for the kids at any time, on the kitchen floor, in the park, basement, church pew, anyplace/anywhere/anytime.

Not just anyone can be a real clown. The glamour of being a clown is not in hoping to be rich and buy fancy homes and cars; it's the joy you get from all the smiles you collect. Yes, some clowns do wear Coco Chanel, but to be clear—if they wear earrings or sunglasses or carry a fancy purse from a famous designer, you can be sure it's a knock-off. I learned this when I found these famous CC's on the floor everywhere in our home, fallen from where they'd been glued to an imitation item by some cheap retailer.

So is being a clown seeing the glass as always half full? Maybe it's living the belief that you can't control what happens to you, but you can control how you react to it.

I do believe in a common saying that reminds me of my clown.

Yes, "it is better to have loved and lost than never to have loved at all."

God bless clowns!

....

CHAPTER TWENTY-FIVE

KidsCan! Scoring Touchdowns

"Daddy, will I get cancer now?"

We had checked Pamela in for her first night at Rex Hospital. As we stared in bewilderment at the gray walls in her room, Dr. Crane, her assigned physician, came in to meet us for the first time. Dr. Crane was optimistic yet straight shooting about Pamela's condition. He said her white blood count was so low, he was surprised she hadn't passed out and crashed the van when driving with the kids to the walk-in-clinic earlier that day. He made it clear she had to jump into her chemo treatments—first thing the next morning.

In 24 hours, life had gone from a dream to a nightmare.

After Dr. Crane laid out a simple but urgent process for Pamela to restore her physical health, he said, "I have someone else you need to see."

I thought *Oh, man, what else could be lurking around the corner that he can't handle himself?*

Dr. Crane said, "Pamela and Kevin, you're in the fight of your life, and I know how important your kids are to you. There's a program here at Rex that will help you continue to be great parents to your children, but also let you focus on the fight. I'll have Terri K come see you in the morning. Terri runs a program that will help you deal with the children through this unfamiliar time."

After meeting with Terri K two days later, she passed the ball to the KidsCan! program to teach our kids about chemotherapy and the cancer that had stricken their mom. Equally important, they would teach me how to quarterback my family through what had become a game of life. If you win and make it through, you move on in life, if you fail and fall apart there is so much at risk, including life itself.

That first morning at Rex, chemo went to work to save Pamela's life. That same week, KidsCan! went to work to save our family. No matter how young they are, children need answers to their many questions. How do you explain leukemia to a three-year-old? How do you tell a one-year-old who's been attached to his mommy his whole life why she now has no hair? How do you explain to a five-year-old who's much smarter than we want to admit that his mom has this dreadful disease, then look him right in the eye and assure him she'll be alright—when you can't even look at yourself in the mirror and answer that question?

I'll tell you how. In the same way I trusted my football team in high school and college, you trust in your team. You take a leap of faith when your faith has been stripped and tested like no other time in your life. Why the football analogies? Because the life experience, generosity, and love of two famous football players are the backbone and foundation of KidsCan!, The cancer support program at Rex Hospital for parents and their children.

On Kevin Patrick's bedroom wall you'll still see a #88 football jersey. Next to it on a shelf is an NFL figurine of a wide receiver for the St. Louis Rams making a touchdown catch. Below that is an autographed N.C. State Wolf Pack ball cap. These are from two brothers who played a combined twenty plus years in the NFL. One played wide receiver who caught his way to multiple trips to the NFL Pro-Bowl and topped his career off as a major contributor on a Super Bowl championship team. Ironically his brother spent his entire NFL career as a defensive back tasked with the assignment of stopping players like his brother from scoring touchdowns.

As professional athletes in the NFL, the brothers had opposite responsibilities on the field. Off the field, they had one aligned vision. They wanted to make a difference in the lives of kids because of their own experience with cancer's disruption of their family.

These two gifted athletes grew up in the Carolinas and both played football at North Carolina State University, located just 20 minutes from where we live in Raleigh. It may have been their financial success in the NFL that helped them create a charitable foundation whose signature program is KidsCan!, but it was long before the NFL that KidsCan! was their divine calling. When the boys were in high school/college their mom was stricken with cancer. Typical of parents back then, certain hardships were hidden from their kids. I guess for that generation it was considered a noble act to protect children from growing up too fast. I recall a story they shared one night to a room full of kids ranging from three years old to a sixteen-year-old teenager. They replayed receiving the unexpected and sudden news when they were in high school and college that their mother had suddenly passed away. The boys hadn't known she was ill. It wasn't until later they found out from their father that their mom had battled cancer for some time.

I could only imagine the weight of the many emotions the brothers must have felt at the time. Were they torn by sorrow, anger, and confusion over the sudden loss of their mother? Or did they wrestle with mistrust and hurt, knowing they could have spent months, even years, helping and spending more time with their mother if they'd known she was battling a life-threatening disease? And what a burden their father must have carried both during his wife's fight to live and after she passed away.

Those life-altering moments affected the boys in an unshakeable way. They were living with a self-awareness that hiding the difficult reality of their mother's illness hurt more than if their father had let them share in their parents' life-threatening adversity. In their hearts was a desire to change how parents handle the seriousness and the unpredictability cancer can bestow on a mother, father, or grandparent. You can hear their drive to help children when cancer strikes a family, as they stress the importance of educating parents and arming them with the tools, confidence, and guidance to talk to their kids with sensitivity and honesty.

Their vision paid off by putting their childhood experience out there for everyone to learn from. KidsCan! saved my family. KidsCan! gave Pamela and me the guidance and confidence to answer our kids' questions. Your children deserve to know the answers as much as adults do, but they need to hear it in a way a one-, three-, or five-year-old can comprehend. Priests, teachers, and school counselors may be equipped to handle the peer pressures of a child's everyday life, but explaining that life and death hang in the balance weekly, almost daily with cancer—that's a master's degree only a program like KidsCan! will deliver.

It's a difficult experience to take your young children, shaken and confused by this nightmare, and ask them to follow you into their first KidsCan! group session. Then moments later, you walk out leaving your kids alone with some counselor or volunteer you just met. You're not sure how you find the confidence to do it, but you do. You do it because, with what little faith you may have left in this world, you hope when that doctor said, "Let KidsCan! help you," you could risk trusting your new teammates. You trust that the group leaders will say the right things to your kids, and then teach you the right way to handle those dreadful questions as your innocent children see the effects of a parent struggling through chemotherapy.

"Daddy, why does mommy have cancer?"

"Why can't mommy come home tonight?"

"Daddy, will I get cancer now?"

KidsCan! gave me the tools and confidence to handle these questions. Terri K.. and her team shared their experience of working with children for more than twenty years. They know how a one-, three-, and five-year-old thinks. They know what kind of questions to expect. Unfortunately, they also know that when parents avoid preparing their children and don't answer their questions, children come up with their own answers. I now know the answers kids make up are usually much worse than the reality. I recall hearing the story of a five-year-old boy who thought for years he gave his father cancer because the boy had stayed home from school with the flu the day before he found out his dad had the disease. A teenage girl, who'd overheard only bits and pieces about her mom's leukemia, kept secret from her parents for months that she'd started her menstrual periods—because she assumed it was a blood cancer.

Many high school and college graduates stop by Terri K's office every year to say hi and pay their respects to one of the special women who helped them get through those tough years. These young adults don't come back because their parents have fallen out of remission. They come back because many of them were as young as my kids when cancer hit their family. They come back to say hi to Terri K, to show their appreciation for the great work she and the KidsCan! team did for them. And they come back to let Terri K know not only are they okay and doing well in school, but also mom or dad is still feeling great and healthy as ever.

Pamela was not one of the lucky ones. Chemotherapy fell down on the job of saving her life. But KidsCan! did its job, thanks to people like Terri K and the inspiration of two brothers. After Pamela passed away I was scared to face my faith, fearful that my searching for answers to "Why us?" would leave me empty and hopeless. Then a new definition of "why" hit my soul. I realized all Pamela would have wanted is to love and help children.

When we requested that people send donations in her name to the KidsCan! program at Rex Hospital, many friends, neighbors, strangers, classmates, and even the UPS driver donated. Donations rolled in, from ten dollars to a hundred dollars, and sometimes much more—over $30,000 in donations in Pamela's memory. The KidsCan! organizers reached out to me with an idea to create an educational video with the funds, for hospitals that don't have such a program, and school systems that have hundreds of kids in class with parents battling cancer. The list is long of those who could benefit.

After thousands had seen the KidsCan! real-life documentary of how to cope and parent through chemo and cancer, I realized Pamela's spirit had answered *why*.

If those donations to KidsCan! in her memory saved one person from depression, or changed a lack of faith into confidence to parent through cancer, or if they save one child from falling apart in the confusion of what was happening to their mother or father, then Pamela might be the reason KidsCan! saves even one family, as the inspiration of two men's faith saved our family.

As much as losing Pamela hurts, there is a reason *why* three children don't get to see their mom again. Through all the pain and tears my kids still skip, jump, laugh, love, and find some peace and solitude in their loss, thanks to the support of KidsCan! If you ask them about cancer, their mom, and KidsCan! they'll probably tell you they miss their mommy and wish she didn't have to go to heaven so soon, but her pain and the cancer died that day, too, and that makes their confusion feel okay. Now I can move on and be at peace, knowing I can explain *why* to Christopher, Amanda and Kevin.

Thanks to KidsCan! I have no regrets about how Pamela and I handled her eleven months fighting off leukemia.

But one bit of remorse does sting me at times. When Pamela was in the hospital, it could be a little much to handle all three children with their energetic personalities in a tiny hospital room. Our patient was often hooked up to a machine receiving blood transfusions, so I'd often rotate visits with the kids. The last week Pamela was in the hospital I brought Christopher first to visit her, and the next day Amanda. I leaned on the fact that Kevin Patrick was older and could be more patient waiting his turn. That was tough because also at his age he was the most vocal about his heartbreak the morning Pamela packed to head off to the hospital for her aggressive new dose of chemo. Kevin Patrick, or K.P. as we called him, had to wait a few days longer than we anticipated. Pamela had to cancel visiting with him two days in a row because she was incoherent from heavy doses of morphine. She didn't want the kids to see her in such a fuzzy state.

Telling this story still overwhelms me. Even as I sit on this packed airplane writing this story, my heart is pounding and my eyes fighting back tears. I have trouble catching my breath. Kevin was patient; unfortunately his patience and Pamela's morphine caused him to miss his last chance to see his mom. She never made it home that week. A sudden infection raged through her system early one morning, and she passed away by the afternoon.

I need to pause for a moment. I am starting to catch my breath.

I have no regret, but I do have a deep remorse knowing we pushed off Kevin's visit not once, but twice that week. "Sorry, pal, Mommy is too sick today to visit. I promise, tomorrow; you know she can't wait to see you."

Revisiting such events makes me think of those two boys and the strength of their parents. I pray that none of them ever have to wait long to catch their breath when the anxiety sets in that like Kevin, they lost the chance to say their good-byes to their mom. Things were definitely different back then. I am fairly certain most of the parents I knew and respected in my teenage years would have handled things exactly the same way. Right or wrong, one thing is for certain, their father shouldn't have any regrets. Because of how his boys were raised, aligned with God-given talents they had the soul to give back, and now hundreds of parents like me live with no regret.

I hope one day I get the chance to express my gratitude to them directly. Parenting is tough enough, but to do it through cancer, or after cancer has taken a parent's life, is just a playbook I honestly did not think could exist. My children and I are in debt to those brothers for stopping parents like me from dropping the ball, because I would have been unprepared to handle cancer and fatherhood at the same time. To their parents I would say "You sure did one heck of a job leaving some of the world's most impressive men behind to pass on your memory."

A friend of mine once told me, "Kevin, sometimes we just don't get to know why." Today, thanks to KidsCan!, the McAteers carry on the faith that maybe this time we do know why.

....

TWENTY-SIX

Three Letters You Never Want to be on the Receiving End Of

*KidsCan! was a physiological set of encyclopedias to help me answer
so many of my kid's questions. Except one...*

As young toddlers our brains help us begin to develop our grunts and moans into clear, articulate words. Most parents hang on to a memory, thinking that first word they heard their baby utter with a mouth full of mashed green beans was actually, "Muuummm." Maybe it was the morning Fido the family dog bit their little angel on the toe and he yelped out, "Dahhh!" Can't you hear the proud father yelling to his wife, "Honey, he just called my name, he just said Daddy!" These are fond memories, no matter if real or our imaginations running wild.

If you've ever spent time around young kids, then you know the truly first actual word every toddler first masters: "WHY?"

"Mommy, why can't I have it?"

"Daddy, why can't I go?"

"Why?"

"Why?"

"Whyyyyyy?"

You're probably asking yourself, "Yeah, WHY is that?"

As a parent, if you think back to those early parental discussions with your kids, it's a pretty quick assessment.

"Amanda, WHY did you draw on the wall?"

"Christopher, WHY did you bite your sister?"

"Kevin Patrick, WHY did you not tell me you had to poop?"

These three letters W, H, Y, of all the letters, words, and questions in modern language, seem to be the ones that first grab our emotions as small children. Pondering my teenage and young adult years, thinking of verbal exchanges with my parents, I know why I continue to hate being on the receiving end of those three letters:

"Kevin, why didn't you study for that test last semester?"

"Kevin, why did you lie to me about having friends in the house while we were gone?"

"Kevin, why did you think you wouldn't break a window throwing rocks at the side of the house?"

As we grow into responsible adults, most of us have been taught the philosophy that you learn more from the mistakes you make in life than you do from your successes. After all that, you'd think in our adult life "Why?" would be the easiest question to answer. Not true. As a matter of fact, I've learned that one of the best questions to ask in an interview is "Why?" If you sit silently after asking that question, you'll most likely learn more about the other person than they ever banked on telling you. As someone who's interviewed hundreds of adults in my career and spent ten years investigating three little kids, the lesson certainly stands the test of time.

Ironically, those same three letters are the first question commonly asked when loved ones near their last days on earth with us. When I turned forty, and after Pamela was diagnosed with cancer, I finally figured out that the answer we give to the question "Why" defines us and our values. Asking "Why?" helps us figure out who we are and where we fit in this ever-changing world.

As I mentioned, KidsCan! was a physiological set of encyclopedias to help me logically and emotionally answer so many of my kid's questions in a loving and profound way. Except one... *Why?* It never failed that one of the three children would hit me with a WHY question at bedtime. I often stumbled during those intense moments, answering the most pressured inquisition I'd ever faced. It took a few seconds to gather my thoughts, and explore my beliefs, before responding to those three-letter jabs to the heart. I never replied "No comment," or "I have to confer with my attorney." No, I always told the truth. And because of that we're a better family, an honest and trusting family. Not dodging those three letters has also made me a better man, and for sure I was the best father I could be at that time.

Bedtime was a challenging grand jury testimony and one that tested my mind, body, and strength of soul. As I flicked off the light and gently closed the bedroom door I could feel a rising tide of emotion start in my gut, as if a volcano of tears was close to erupting. I always hoped to get the door completely sealed, but I knew one door each night would get stuck open as if it hit an immovable object. That immovable object was the rock in my heart after hearing in my ear…

"Daddy?"

"Yes?"

"Daddy, why did Mommy get cancer?"

"Daddy, why did Mommy have to die?"

"Daddy, why can't Mommy fly back to see me?"

"Daddy, why does everyone else get to have a Mommy and I don't?"

My children know as much information as I do when it comes to articulating the answers to these questions. No matter your age you have a right to hear the answer, regardless of the pain that could follow the truth.

It's okay as an adult, a teacher, a pastor, and as a parent to sometimes not know the answer to all of life's WHYs, but you still have to muster a response. In those moments my response would be:

"Kids, I know it hurts. It hurts Daddy, too. I know it's not fair, and I'm sorry, but I don't know the Why either."

Then you say good night, you tell them Mommy and Daddy love them, and without their noticing, you rush to shut that door so you can hide down the hallway to break down and sob. In that moment in the dark, when you're all alone, you look up to the heavens and like a child ask the Father:

"WHY?"

CHAPTER TWENTY-SEVEN

Quotes I'll Never Forget

"Amanda, what do you want to be when you grow up?"

Questions can be wearing, but quotes are everlasting. We all have famous quotes that stick with us through life. They might be something a parent always told us or a teacher's philosophy that made a lasting impression. As much as I enjoy hearing the great speeches throughout history, my memories of the most moving quotes come from three young children whose fortitude and innocence for me is everlasting. Let me share with you:

Feeling Lucky

Kevin Patrick and I were returning home from doing some errands. It had been six months since he last got to see his mom. The van was basically silent with some low-volume talk radio drowning out the background noise. As I drove around the sharp corner about a hundred yards into our neighborhood, Kevin unexpectedly broke his silence and at the same time bruised my heart. I carefully shifted my eyes from the road to the rearview mirror to his little innocent face when he said;

"Daddy, at least I'm lucky that I got to know Mommy for eight whole years. Most people only knew Mommy for about a year, and Amanda and Christopher only knew her for a few years. Yeah. I'm really lucky."

Career Choices

Amanda's pre-school was holding a graduation celebration. Attending my four-year-old daughter's pre-school graduation was difficult enough, only months after this little girl's Mommy passed away. Unfortunately the ceremony was also taking place in the church where Pamela's funeral service had been held. As the children ended their set of silly songs that the teachers tried desperately to choreograph, each pre-schooler came forward to receive a diploma, along with a hug from the teacher. Then each of them made an announcement to the room describing what they wanted to be when they grew up. The audience laughed when little Billy said he wanted to be a Transformer. Everyone grinned when hearing the many girls who wanted to be a princess or the boys who desired to be firemen. Then came Amanda's turn. She was reserved until the teacher prompted her. "Amanda, what do you want to be when you grow up?" she asked over the microphone. Amanda replied,

"A mommy."

Do Angels Fly?

Only weeks had passed since Pamela died and bedtime was still very emotional for me. As I tucked each of my kids in to bed to say goodnight, peacefulness always settled over our bedrooms on the second floor. However, each night during any of the three goodnights I'd hear heart-tugging comments from those little voices. Their grieving questions of life and death had seemed to lessen a bit, though I wondered if they held back because they sensed I was trying to answer their questions as best as I could without sounding too sad. For a while all I heard at bedtime was, "Daddy, I love you," or "I miss Mommy." Even those comments choked me up and made it difficult to get out, "I love you, too." Bedtime was very unpredictable, though. Saying "Good night" could be as normal as a tuck in, a kiss, and a smile, or it could be those warming comments that sent chills down my spine. One particular night Christopher—not yet two years old—froze me physically and emotionally. As I turned his lights off and went for the door, he called softly, "Ahhh, Daddy?" One foot away from my hallway sanctuary I turned and looked at his face, lit by the moon's light coming through his window as he stared up at the sky. Never taking his eyes off the stars, he asked,

"When will she fly back, Daddy?"

If You Could be Anyone, Who Would You Be?

As we go through life, there are times when we let down our level of self-confidence and envy someone else's life. It may be someone famous we desire to be like or wish we had their good fortune. It could be we've had a tough week, and notice a friend who always seems uplifted, and we feel jealous, asking what in their life could be so motivating. Rarely do you hear a sincere desire to trade places with someone less fortunate. Lord knows, the days preceding Pamela's death brought a lot of moments I'd gladly have traded with anyone in the world. However, there was one moment when someone blessed with all life had to offer would have gladly traded it for another much less fortunate person.

The events leading up to those final breaths and what transpired shortly thereafter moved very quickly. Pamela's passing was unexpected and sudden, and it was difficult to keep those closest to us informed. Due to the close monitoring of her situation, and my refusal to leave her side, there were only one or two rare opportunities to make a phone call. With each change in diagnosis, I'd usually grab my Blackberry and try to text or email the update to Pamela's father, my parents, and my brother. It was difficult for family to support us with such a rapid turn of circumstances.

My parents had to put a few things in order to make sure when they got to Raleigh from Philadelphia they never had to think about flying back home until it was the right time. They arrived in Raleigh almost exactly forty-eight hours later on a Monday afternoon.

Several members of Pamela's family had already made it to town and many of our local friends had been by to console us or distract the kids from reality. But it was as if a big piece of my soul had not yet been pierced with the harsh reality of losing her. Not until my own flesh and blood arrived to grieve with me. I sat out on our front door steps, knowing my parents would be arriving within the hour. As my Dad pulled in to the top of our long driveway I'd already briefly walked half way up the hill. He immediately pulled over and parked, still several hundred feet from the house, and both doors flew open. I'm not even sure he turned the car off. As I stepped closer to my Dad I felt all my pent-up pain release. I saw only a quick glimpse of his face before we embraced with a tremendous amount of love and hurt. I could not speak. My emotions drowned out any ability to utter a word—all I had were the tears pouring violently down my face. I could feel my Dad equally exploding into a passion of sorrow. And with the highest level of sincerity he said:

"Kevin, I just wish it was me. I wish she could be here right now and God would let me take her place."

....

CHAPTER TWENTY-EIGHT

Dancing on Their Graves

"It's an important day, but unfortunately not a birthday."

"Dancing on someone's grave" usually implies rejoicing in the misfortune of another person's death. So it may come as a shock that the phrase reminds me of where Pamela was laid to rest, more gently known as "Mommy's Spot." How could I connect such a sinister saying with the grave site of the mother of my three children? It's the behavior of Pamela's kids that reminds me, every time I take them to visit her there.

It's not what you might think. They're not being disrespectful, not acting out in a place that brings such sorrow for visitors. Quite the contrary. Visit along with us—it will only take you minutes to get the picture. Let me play back our visit to the cemetery on a day itself that's difficult enough: February 17th, the anniversary of Pamela's passing. Each year on this date we do more than pick up fresh flowers on our way to Mommy's Spot. On this anniversary I place an order with a florist for several bags of loose rose petals. With February 17th falling this year on a Thursday, I get the kids out of school a few hours early so we can reach the cemetery before dark.

When we arrive at the florist, I run into the same situation that has occurred every year on this date. First, the florist has plenty of loose petals from the dozens and dozens of roses not sold three days earlier for Valentine's Day. Second, the florist returns from the back of the store with our bags of petals and says, "Wow, it must be a special day for someone."

I try not to embarrass the manager, especially with the kids listening, and evasively reply each year, "Yes it's an important day."

Then, without fail, the florist can't let it go: "Is it someone's birthday, or anniversary? What's the special occasion?"

You'd think after the third straight year they'd put a note in our file reminding them so I don't have the uncomfortable position of answering each year as all three kids stare at how Daddy will handle this one.

"It's an important day, but unfortunately not a birthday—it's the day Mommy went to heaven. So we're going to spread some rose petals for her at her spot."

Boy, do I want to crawl under a rock each time this happens. I'm not sure if I feel worse for me or the florist.

As usual, we don't get out of the flower shop with just the rose petals. This year the kids have picked out small ceramic angels resembling each of them to leave at her spot. Oh, and somehow they find candy for sale—at a florist shop. Sigh.

When we reach Mommy's Spot, the four of us throw rose petals over the ground where we imagine her coffin was lowered, as though we've laid a blanket over a bed for her. The kids each do this with joy, as if to show in this gesture of remembrance how much it means to be Pamela's son or daughter. Then, within seconds, as they have every year, the three of them sprint off running around Pamela's memorial, hiking up the steep hill and rolling down the hill with constant laughter in their voices. They take turns jumping over each other, stumbling on each other, giggling and playing. Then they take one last run to the top of the hill where large statues of saints stand looking over those who have been laid to rest. They each fill their hands with pieces of the tree bark mulch, chasing each other down the hill, trying to peg each other with the mulch. Whatever mulch doesn't make it to one of their heads of hair they place around the stone at the head of Pamela's spot.

As I step back and watch this taking place, I'm amazed. I've learned to let go of my parental policeman badge, which would never stand for such carrying on in the house or the aisles of Target. Instead I let my mind drift outside of myself. I smile, cry, and—on this rare occasion—congratulate myself for raising three kids who have the strength, the love, and the enthusiasm to find hope in life by running, jumping, and dancing with their Mom. In these moments, in the last place they saw her and said goodbye by placing a white rose on her casket, it's clear to me they're truly back to say, "Hi mommy, come play with us one more time so we can just play in your new front yard".

....

CHAPTER TWENTY-NINE

Ground Us

Your generous gift was one that helped us "ground" our grief.

Two months had passed since the kids and I lost Pamela. Although we weren't used to our new lives, we got a glance of what changes would one day be normal in our world. Most volunteers had now punched out and returned to their own lives and family demands. Acts of kindness that had been a daily routine, like an evening meal being dropped off or a care package of toys, had appropriately slowed down. Those who cooked or cleaned or ran errands were now on the family payroll, and had our wellbeing as an official component of their weekly job description. In a way it was settling as a man and father to know the caring donations of time, love, and costly goods had come to a close, so I could discover if I was able to manage on my own (with a small roster of affordable support, of course). In my eyes it was also good for the kids to recognize generosity and gifts from others that were gestures of support and not a replacement for losing Pamela. It's hard to use the word "spoil" when describing three innocent kids whose daily lives had been stripped of their mother's love, but we were headed in that direction when the Easter Bunny seemed to have ridden in on a sleigh of eight tiny reindeer.

With Easter behind us, it was time to look forward as best as possible. As months passed, part of that process meant to work to find healthy and positive ways to maintain Pamela's memory in the children's minds. One afternoon when I was working from home my boss, Bob, called and asked if I was going to be around the house the next few days. He said Richard, who is 50% owner of our company, was sending something to the house. It seemed odd that Richard would be sending something months after that type of generosity had ceased, especially since the company, and Richard, had done so much for our family. Something told me to not inquire what it was or ask Bob why it was coming at this time. I was just starting to find my way with work and was happy he wasn't sending a pink slip.

That Friday afternoon, as I sat in the dining room pounding away at my laptop and watching for the shadow of the school bus through the window, a large pick-up truck came roaring down my driveway. It didn't take long to realize it was a landscaping company. What did take a while to understand was why they were not turning around, assuming they had the wrong address. As you can guess, they had the right address, the right family, and Richard had the right uncanny timing! The truck was dropping off a large tree, a tree that was a gift from Richard and his wife, Denise. A tree that would forever be named the "Mother's Day Tree" and forever strengthen our ability to make it through this difficult date on the kids' calendar every year.

Somehow, Richard and Denise had the touching inclination that the right gift for us was a tree we could plant in Pamela's honor at her home. They hoped the tree might help us celebrate her life on that first Mother's Day without her. Denise started this tradition after she lost her older brother when he was only 21 years young. Richard embraced this spirit-filled tribute when he planted a tree in front of his office to keep alive the memory of his brother who had passed away too early.

I don't know how another human being has such insight into one's heart struggling with an awful loss. The common person would send maybe a gift basket, or offer some way to give us a few hours of calm in a daily roller coaster of emotions. I had circled many dates on the calendar and considered what traditions would be healthiest for us to embrace in an effort to feel peace on these milestone dates. But how do you attach to a tradition without your heart aching in pain? How do you connect to that specific day if you're the children, knowing it reminds you that you had a mother you cannot hug, cannot touch, cannot see, and cannot grow with anymore? Then Richard and Denise found a way and blessed us with their caring intuition.

Rather than explain how this simple gift changed our lives, I'll share a letter I finally sent to Richard and Denise after celebrating five consecutive years of Mother's Day without Pamela:

December 26, 2011
Dear Richard and Denise,
You had always told me anytime I felt I needed I could call you. Well consider this letter a ringing of the phone. A call to just say thank you.

Richard. Upon leaving the President's Award dinner this past March I was touched emotionally like one would feel when leaving church on Sunday morning. As the night closed, there you were standing on stage delivering the evening's closing message to hundreds of Concord's leaders. Your words, as every year, helped each of us in the room feel a part of something so much bigger than a corporation that takes pride on its business accomplishments. You reminded all of us how special life can feel when connecting with the people we serve but also those who serve alongside us. With your unique candor and heart-driven conviction, you made the point to keep ourselves "grounded." On a night like this where we recognize not only business results, but more importantly, those individuals who raise the communities we live and work in, it leaves us a sense that we have a purpose larger than life. On a night like this your simple words find a unique way to "ground us."

I'll never be able to articulate what was going through my head driving from the Renaissance Hotel to my driveway that night, but all I could think about was "Grounded." As I headed down Six Forks Road in a daydreaming daze, something about your actions many years ago caught back up with me. It once again touched my heart, and on this night made me pause to recollect how lucky the kids and I are to be connected to the Concord family, and to your family.

I couldn't wait to get home, climb the stairs, and get a peek at each of my little roommates sleeping in their beds with that look of loving innocence. Then, as I roamed the house, picking up and turning off lights for the night, a memory of the Mother's Day Tree you sent the children and me closed in on my conscience. These are the thoughts that went through my mind:

How your generous gift was one that helped us "ground" our grief and our loving memory of Pamela.

How Pamela was a true source of "grounding" to us as a family.

How the Mother's Day tree has been a living symbol, allowing us to plant roots into the ground, emotionally moving us to continue to live life, even with their mother no longer within their reach.

Since that first Mother's Day when we had to endure Pamela's loss, and every one since then, the children stand in front of that tree showing that our roots are forever grounded here. Although a part of us has been raised to the heavens, our yearly photo taken on this special day is an example that Kevin Patrick, Amanda, and Christopher continue to grow as does Pamela's memory and her place in our lives. No matter how big they get, because of the Mother's Day Tree, we can continue to visualize how their honor for her grows right alongside them.

It has been several years now that I routinely kick myself after Mother's Day for not sending a card and a recent picture of us at the tree. Frankly the chaos and busyness of such weeks is no excuse. It's interesting that a moment in the month of December and not May made me commit to getting this letter out to you before New Year's.

Richard, our lives have changed or I should say evolved, now that I am in a serious relationship and Shayna and her three kids stay with us on and off throughout the year. Although I'm forever driven to keep Pamela's memory in the forefront of the children's minds, there is a sense of respect for a new relationship that causes some picture frames to come down, and new ones to go up. One tradition we had since their mom passed away was always decorating one side of our Christmas Tree in all pink ornaments and garland (Pamela's favorite color) to represent her remembrance on one of the most special days a mother experiences, watching her children open gifts from the secret Ms. Clause. With Shayna and her kids spending their second year with us during the holiday season, this tradition had naturally fallen aside. However a new one began. This year on Christmas Eve the Mother's Day tree, that in December normally stands bare of color with no leaves or flowered buds, was converted to a spiritual memory of Pamela's life. This year the kids decorated the tree with Christmas ornaments and a faulty attempt at Christmas lights. The tree branches were too weak to hang lights from, so our back-up idea was to shoot a spotlight from its roots to the heavens above. It was really cool at night, as the light would reflect off all the different Christmas balls hanging throughout the base of the tree branches.

These days at bedtime on Christmas Eve the seven-year-old goes to bed still believing in old St. Nick, the nine-year-old tries to hang onto the dream, and the eleven-year-old fakes it just so he can take in every glorious moment of Christmas before it's too late. Normally I can catch each of them staring out the window as I turn off the lights, wondering when Santa might come and going over their mental calendar, wondering if he really has been watching them all year. However this year bedtime was a bit different. Now they looked out the window onto the glowing Mother's Day tree and I shared a story with them of how the tree and its light not only glows upward to notify Santa we're here, but it shines to the heavens to remind Mommy that on this eve of receiving we have not forgotten the gift given to us and those memories of a lifetime.

Richard and Denise, thank you for sending such a treasure five years ago. I can't and won't try to find a way to repay your appreciation and giving us such a monument of Pamela's memory and a way for the children to wrap around new traditions of their ever living love for their mother.

With sincere appreciation and respect from a Friend and Father,
Kevin McAteer

....

CHAPTER THIRTY

To Cry in the Sky

I was probably the only person on the plane who could say the following four words were music to his ears: "Our flight is delayed."

After Pamela's funeral, whenever we were in church I was overcome with sorrow in my heart and therefore uncontrollable leaky faucets in my tear ducts. It was almost three years later before I could make it through an entire mass without rubbing my eyes as they squeezed closed, at least attempting to go unnoticed. Receiving Holy Communion was normally the dam breaker, as I would always go back to my seat and talk to the man upstairs who now was the closest to Pamela. To replace the tears with a smile, I'd imagine God shaking his holy head as he watched her continue to rearrange the patio furniture, and cut colorful flowers outside his pearly gates.

You'd think dealing with three little kids in a church and the aggravating routine of saying, "Shhhh, use your church voice," "Hey, put your feet down," or "I swear to God, if you don't sit still…" might distract me enough to get through sixty minutes without letting my deep belief that Pamela was sitting at the Lord's side, rattle my sadness over losing her. But it didn't. Finally, about a year ago, the expected and unwanted routine of weeping in the Lord's house ceased. It still happens, of course, but not every single week. Not that we get to mass every week, but we try.

Surprisingly, the same unintended tradition occurring at Sunday mass was happening to me during my business trips. This may sound self-promoting, but I must say there's nothing unmanly about a man who cries in public, and it's definitely okay to cry when flying in the sky.

Maybe that's why United Airlines came up with the slogan "Fly the Friendly Skies." (Although I have to digress and make one comment after watching so many fellow business travelers handle the rigors of travel: "For God's sake, gentlemen, stop your whining about not having enough leg room." It's just not necessary, and frankly very unmanly.)

Flying has never been stressful for me. With one exception: trying to fly with three kids, on my own, knowing one has a propensity to barf before the trip ends. On business trips I never sweat the small stuff or get worked up over things out of my control. My Uncle Pat had the best travel attitude that ever has been passed down. He and Aunt Linda would always be the last ones to board, even if they were the first ones at the gate. He'd wait until the attendants announced, "This is the last call for passengers on Flight ### to board." His philosophy was, "Why get on board any earlier than you have to? They're not going to give your seat away and certainly not going to upgrade you. So wait in the open air of the terminal rather than spend one extra minute in that confined tube."

When it came to taking my first several road trips and leaving the kids behind with Grandma and babysitters, travel took on a whole new face for me. You can imagine the demands of being a widower father at that time in my life. When setting out for a trip I'd make sure I had all my T's crossed and I's dotted, as best as I could. I wanted to focus on the job at hand without worrying if the kids were going to open up their lunch bag to find it empty, not get to their after-school activities or forget to complete their homework. My trips were never very long, so the task of coverage was not as intense as it could have been. Bedtime could be a real emotional time for the kids and me, but most trips only lasted one or two bedtimes (when Pamela passed I stopped counting my trips in nights; it came down to whether or not I was going to be home to say goodnight and tuck them in). I frankly enjoyed the break of travel; it was a much needed, refreshing feeling of control from the monopoly that raising the kids had in my life. On the road I could only do so much for the kids, and if I had the right people watching them, there was very little parenting for me to do. As a matter of fact, traveling became my sanctuary, my battery recharge. I probably was the only person on a plane who could say the following four words were music to his ears: "Our flight is delayed." Ahhh, the sweet sound of being all alone in a crowded airplane.

Not that traveling for my job wasn't work, but it was the type of high-level, corporate-type challenge I needed as a distraction from the reality back home. I can recall a few times at a hotel visit coming down in the morning and the sales team waiting to meet with me. I know they always wondered how I was doing, not being at home with the kids the night before as I slept alone in their hotel room.

I'd always break the ice with an easy response to their first question:

"Good morning Kevin, how did you sleep last night?"

"It was so nice that your front desk clerk and housekeeper didn't wake me up in the middle of the night, asking me to get them apple juice. Not that I'm not used to that type of middle of the night wakeup call, but I'm not sure I could have found the juice at 3 am in the chef's kitchen."

The staff would giggle and at the same time understand "I was okay," and I think quickly they got the picture that the road for a short trip seemed like a healthy situation for me and my children.

Flying gave me unusual moments of pleasure. For example, I was the passenger who wanted to sit behind the mom with kids climbing all over her and messing her hair up, her husband two seats away completely overwhelmed, wondering if 8 am was a bad time to start drinking Bloody Marys as his little son with boogers coming down his face tossed his baseball cap down the aisle. Man, I was in paradise, because those kids were not mine. The only thing more relaxing was watching businessmen who'd board the plane all grumpy and aggravated that someone put their bag in the overhead compartment instead of under their seat. It was like watching everyone get a piece of Kevin McAteer's life, my everyday reality.

My turn would come, though, but in a different kind of wrapping paper. On my return flights after the job was complete and business objectives had been tackled, it was now time to fly back to my roommates waiting for me at home. That's when happiness would receive a punch square in the face. That's also why I stopped requesting the aisle seat on my return flights and started begging for the window seat. Tearing up was expected in church, but I was never prepared for what would happen in the air. I guess I should have known better, since being front and center of some of the world's greatest creations has always tugged at my soul. Ever since I was a little kid you could find me standing at the edge of the Jersey shore, gazing out at the view of an endless canvas of deep water. It didn't matter if the sun was setting, rising, or a storm was raging in, it was breathtaking to close out the world for a moment, look into the watercolor painting of the ocean, and try to understand in a primitive way why it stopped at my feet in the sand. That connection with one of the world's great mysteries is very similar to being thousands of miles in the air and staring out my window seat at the massive, white, sculpture-like clouds, wondering if I'm truly in the heavens. If not, how much farther away could they be? That intellectual and emotional collision, as I sat in a crowded tube, would touch my spiritual side, and bring on an overwhelming feeling of mortality. The great

Atlantic Ocean and the awe of the eternal clouded heavens makes me feel as close to God as physically possible.

That sensory feeling of flying caught me completely off guard as a continuous connection to the love and loss of Pamela. For the first time in all my years of travel, I stared out the window seat and it linked me to a soul that had left me too early and to my three little angels awaiting my return. On those flights, whether I was engaged in finishing a work project before landing or bouncing my head to heavy metal on my iPod, I'd stare out the window and, unannounced, the deepest vessels of my heart would sting as reality jabbed at the wounds of my grief. I'd instantly tighten my eyes closed, as if I were a plumber twisting a wrench with all his might, hoping to close that leaky valve shut. I knew I had to let go of my heartache. I would inconspicuously look down at my arm rest, wipe my eyes, and again peer out into the never-ending sky, letting my mind drift to the heavens where my best friend now rested.

Before we'd land I would always find it within myself to smile through the tears, because no matter how bad it hurt, I knew Pamela was free of pain and she was somewhere so glorious it was outside our human ability to comprehend. I also knew that back in Raleigh there'd be something special waiting for me at the end of the driveway. Behind the steamed-up glass storm door were three loyal loved ones waiting to shove the door open and run out in their pajamas, anxious to yell, "Daddy's here. Daddy's here! Daddy, you're home."

So the next time you're stressed out and on a plane that feels like your worst nightmare, because little Cindy in her ponytails is crying and kicking your seat, or Grandma Maggie shoves her shopping bags over the top of your now wrinkled suit coat, please don't whine. If the stewardess' tone is a little impatient because it's the fifth time she asked you to turn off your phone, please don't shoot her a look of disgust. When you're in the air, hunger pains spearing your ribcage because you're still waiting for the world's smallest bag of peanuts, don't get irritated if you look over and see this business man in his forties with a happy smirk on his face and a stress-less composure. That man is probably me. If you look again before landing, you may find him staring out the window hiding his crying face. It's nothing to worry about. I'm not crying because life is getting to me. I'm smiling through some teardrops brought on by the sight of our mortality in the rain clouds. Those tears are not from sweating the small stuff. No, they're from embracing the big stuff!

CHAPTER THIRTY-ONE

I Used to Dream

Cancer took it all away.

I used to dream about the future, the past, the present.
I used to wrap memories of the past around myself like a warm blanket.
When I thought of the present my heart would almost pound out of my chest
with thoughts of how fortunate and lucky I was.
The future was so dreamy, knowing I was living a fantasy day by day;
it was so heaven-like
it seemed like someone else's life.
Cancer took it all away.
Now I can hardly see past the next day.
The past settles in with grief, yet at times I smile through tears of pain
because of what I once had.
The present no longer feels calm, finishing the work of two, alone inside,
even though so many are helping outside.
There is no future to dream of; I can't even fantasize what might be for my children,
the future stops about 24 hours ahead of where I am today.
Now I realize to dream is to love.
Love is to fantasize about today and dream how glorious the future can be,
then wrap the memories
created with another around you like a warm blanket,
protecting you from the reality of the present.
That is love, that is why love is so great, that is what is missing in my life.
Am I happy? Can I love?
Not like I used to, not the way love really is.
Because cancer took my dreams away—for now anyway—
life's dream only lasts for today.
How great it was to be in love and never realize I was living a dream!

....

CHAPTER THIRTY-TWO

It's Time to Date

"I was not looking to find a girlfriend and I knew I wasn't ready to be a boyfriend."

It had been five months since I was cursed with the honorary title *widower*. I had recently started to answer people differently when they asked me, "How are you doing?" I had moved the script from "I'm day to day" to now responding, "I'm doing okay." I really was okay. I wasn't feeling "good" and I definitely wasn't "doing great." I had been back at work for months, back to traveling in a way that was healthy for both the kids and myself, and had gotten the kids through the remainder of the school year, never sending anyone off to school without their lunch or leaving them stranded at the bus stop. The bills were paid; the house, believe it or not, looked as neat and clean as any other home with three roommates under the age of eight. I was definitely tired emotionally, mentally, and often physically, but somehow each day I was doing more than just surviving, I was doing okay.

One thing, however, was overwhelming my life and I knew if I didn't find a way to change it I'd most likely begin to go backwards, either in my career or—more importantly—as the CEO of the McAteer Home. That one thing was adult companionship. I don't mean adult interaction. I mean companionship. I would work all day, which was rewarding for sure, but work is still work. Then I'd race home, quickly exchange notes and current events with Christina, as I was bum-rushed by three sprinting kids, who would put on an instant press conference where all three little voices would talk all at one time to tell me about their day, then ask me one million questions. Their goal was obvious, an attempt to secure some Daddy time, either one-on-one or three-on-one to watch kids' shows, play board games, or go outside and play ball or tag like the little rascals. Then responsible Dad would race the clock to make sure we took care of their 3-B's: Bath without drowning, Brush their choppers, and Bedtime with a little reading. After that obstacle course I'd pay bills, read school folders, and before my eyeballs rolled out of my head leave notes to all those who'd take shifts with the kids over the next few days. Then, if I was lucky, I'd steal a much needed hour to stare at the TV and fall into someone else's life on the tube.

I not only needed some "me" time, I needed to interact on a personal, fun level with someone who was more than three feet tall. I also needed that companionship with an adult who wouldn't feel responsible to find out if I was "okay," or want to inquire "How can I help?" In my heart I was not really looking to date, but I will tell you I sure missed sitting on the couch with someone my own age and just laughing at a funny movie or sitting on the deck with a couple glasses of wine, bullshitting about fixing the world, and not fixing the loss of a loved one.

Then one week, on a Monday, I received a sign. Not a sign from God, but a sign from the voice speaking out of the radio. I had a trip to Toronto and was in my car driving off to the airport, listening to sports radio, when a commercial caught my attention:

"Are you single and a busy executive with important job deadlines, or maybe do you juggle a job that requires you to travel and have plenty of personal responsibilities waiting for you each time you come home?"

AH, YEAH YOU'RE TALKING ABOUT ME.

"Are you looking to go out on a date and share some fun but don't have the time to arrange one or even find a person to go out with? Do you need a personal life executive assistant to handle this for you and make sure if you end up with someone you don't like, you don't have to deal with the pressure and uncomfortable feeling of how to end the date and avoid rejecting the person?"

HELLL, YAHHHH. YOU'RE TALKING TO ME.

The radio spot ended with, "Then just call us, call It's Just Lunch, the new professional dating service for busy professionals who don't have time to find dates, set up dates, and don't want to waste their money or time on a bad date. Call It's Just Lunch today and we will take care of everything for you. And the best part is all you have to commit to is JUST LUNCH."

I never paid attention to a dating service in my life but thought, *Wow that is one awesome business model they have there.* Minutes later I was at the airport and "work-guy" mode took over. I quickly forgot the commercial.

As we boarded the plane and everyone finally buckled up, the pilot announced a traffic jam on the runway so we would not be departing on time. I was on a connecting flight from Raleigh to Toronto and the first leg was pretty short so I hadn't brought much work or reading material for the first plane. I became bored and, unusual for me, picked up the complementary airline magazine that sits in everyone's seat pocket. I was glancing at the pages when I saw it…a two-page ad for It's Just Lunch. Not only did it do a great job of attracting the attention of this Hotel Sales and Marketing guy, but the advertisement also featured all the cities where It's Just Lunch does business. Two things came to mind right away. The first was, *Wow, if I was too busy to date at home I could go catch a movie or dinner on the road in one of the many cities where It's Just Lunch does business. How cool.* My immediate second thought was,—*Man they have a serious marketing budget to get me on the radio and now print advertising all in one day. They have to be doing something right.*

I went on with my trip, which lasted two bed-times, and by the time I boarded the plane to return to Raleigh I'd visited eight hotel sales teams in two-and-a-half days. My head was full of work follow-up and my heart full of wanting time with my kids. It's Just Lunch at that time in my life was Out to Lunch, and out of my mind. I was back home and back in the routine of kid morning duty, work duty, kid dinner-time duty, kid bedtime duty, homeowner/parent follow-up duty, pass-out-and-do-it-again duty. A day later, on Thursday, I left work to take a quick drive to the Chick-fil-A for some drive-through lunch. During that 10-minute trip I not only got lunch but darn if the It's Just Lunch promo didn't come over the radio again, saying all the right things. Three times in one week, in two different countries, on the radio and in a magazine? Come on! That's when I figured it was a sign. And since it was at the right time in my life and in my process of healing, I had to reach out. The next day I was sitting in the It's Just Lunch offices signing a dating agreement.

Over the next several months I went on several dates, most of them lunch dates and almost none of them moved to a dinner date. Although this didn't amount to much of anything, relationship-wise, it did help me out with a few things. First, it helped me remember I'm a man, a good man, and one who—when I'm ready—people will be attracted to. Second, it helped me baby step into how I would or could date for myself. For me, this meant not bringing the kids into the circle, because I was not looking to find a "girlfriend" and I knew I wasn't ready to be a "boyfriend."

It's Just Lunch wound up to be It's Too Expensive and not all that great at picking matches. I dropped out of the dating game after a few months, but eventually had the same needs of getting excited about the possibility of spending a night with someone older than a first grader and would jump back into it. The second time around I was motivated, or I should say devastated, by an eHarmony commercial that caught my attention while packing late on Sunday night. It wasn't the couples who made me emotional, it was the price. I could join eHarmony for the amount of money I'd rolled up in my gym shorts and I got to choose who I chatted with. How much did I spend on It's Just Lunch? Let's just say I got taken to more than lunch; I got taken to the proverbial cleaners.

The lesson I learned was it's okay to date, and it's okay to date on your terms. When you're in your thirties or forties and divorce or disease has left you alone, nothing has changed in who you are and what you need in order to be fulfilled. Sure, grief, sorrow, respect, and honor for your wife or husband fill that hole but at the end of the day if you're going to get out of bed more than once to make some pancakes, you'd better trade some of that out for fun, companionship, laughter, bonding, intimacy, and self-confidence in your manhood or becoming that attractive woman again. Those pancake meals are just as healthy as those that see you through the grieving process. Like many other steps in surviving the loss of a loved one, everyone's situation and process is unique, so remember, deciding when you're ready is up to you, and not for the neighbors, in-laws or coworkers to decide.

I do think people can go into the dating game carelessly, and most likely that mistake will cause more pain. I had to consider an awful lot before I determined I was ready. I was married for almost ten years with not one moment of regret during our time together. I didn't want to start waking up with regret within the first year I was alone. So much to consider, *What if I do meet someone I like, and want to have over to watch a movie? How would that affect the kids?* Too much possible drama there, I didn't need a neighbor cornering me at the pool asking if I'd like to go out with one of their single friends, then bug me if I was going to call her back. Dating wasn't for anyone else, it was for me, it was something I knew I needed at the time, so I sure didn't need some PTA mom in an unhappy marriage gossiping inaccurately about my dating habits since my wife passed.

When I dated, and how I dated, was very good for me. It gave me a little more energy and a little more self-confidence that things would be alright. It didn't change how hard I grieved for the love of my life and it didn't change my inability to see myself in love again. The only drawback to any of my decisions on dating was the negative impact on my wallet for not shopping dating service prices in advance. Now I know, the hard way, how It's Just Lunch got such a large marketing budget.

"Thanks for nothing!"

CHAPTER THIRTY-THREE

It's Still a Holiday

*The decision not to celebrate the holidays because of
our son's death was simply the wrong choice.*

My life reminded me of the movie "Groundhog Day" where Bill Murray played a weatherman who would wake up each morning and go through twenty-four hours of what seemed like the same day. I guess the one significant difference was the weatherman always forecasted five or seven days ahead of time. Not only did I live twenty-four hours at a time but it was hard to see much farther out than the next morning. Quickly I realized I had to think farther out for a series of fast approaching dates: Pamela's birthday on May 20th, and then Kevin Patrick's birthday on June 2nd.

I had to figure out how to handle the emotions of the children, extended family, as well as my own. I was particularly worried about Kevin's birthday. The previous year Pamela had been deep in her treatments and had to miss his party at the bowling alley. Amanda and Christopher were lucky enough to have Mommy home for their big days. I wrestled with the fact that Kevin missed his mom on his birthday the previous year and was the one child who didn't get to visit her that last week in the hospital. *How would he react to what seemed like a Strike Three to the heart?* I had to find a way to cut through my remorse and sorrow and think clearly, not only about these upcoming events but all holidays, especially those you can't hide from like Thanksgiving and Christmas.

This was definitely a time to call on Terri K at Rex Hospital and get a more clear perspective on what I should do and—most important—what would be best for the kids. When we met, Terri K and I talked about finding a way to search for who we were as a family of four. One healthy idea was to start new traditions that would create new memories and help define the four of us. Life can't always be about the past, and a solid first step of healing was to have strength to know Pamela would want us to move on, and knowing that having new traditions was not a symbol of forgetting what once was.

We started a new tradition on Pamela's birthday that would prove to be the start of rebuilding this family of four, laid on the foundation of when there were five! On her birthday, we fill the car with the number of balloons that represent her age and let them go fly at mommy's spot. The kids write notes to her on the balloons with a magic marker then let each one go to see whose will disappear first in the heavenly sky. At night on Mother's day, we watch home movies with Pamela in them, which brings laughter from the little ones and a few trips to the bathroom for me to catch my breath. The traditions go on and on, some have changed over the years and some remain as staples of keeping her memory alive.

I didn't realize how genuinely healthy and positive our way of handling the holidays were until attending our annual sales conference. As Vice President of Sales for our company, one of my roles is to host an annual, three-day meeting where we gather sales leaders from our over 80 hotels for celebration, learning, networking, and some type of community-focused project.

That year, one of my teammates, Kirsten, thought of a creative way to donate books to a charity. Attendees would bring gently used books their children had outgrown and drop them off when they arrived to the hotel. The books would eventually go to children in need. Kirsten was figuring out where to donate the books when she discovered www.amandathepanda.org

This charitable organization was started by JoAnn Zimmerman, who lost her daughter, Amanda, at a young age. The nonprofit organization JoAnn started had now grown into a large team of volunteers who hold camps and serve families grieving the loss of a loved one, especially around the holidays. One of their program initiatives is wrapping donated books and other gift items and giving them to families who are trying to find hope and peace as they live through their first Christmas without their recently lost loved ones.

"Amanda the Panda" drops off a box of gifts so there is one to unwrap each day starting on December 1st and leading up to December 24th. The hope is that unwrapping a gift each day and finding some joy in the world will help ease the depression that can descend on a special holiday like Christmas, which for most of us is the happiest day of the year.

Charlie, the woman who represented the organization at our conference, completely moved me when I brought her up on stage to greet our sales leaders and receive our donation of over 250 books. Charlie told a story of a family who had lost a four-year-old son a few months before the holidays. As you can imagine, they were devastated by the loss of such a young child. The family also had a seven-year-old daughter named Jenna. The parents had thought long and hard and agreed they would not celebrate any holidays that year. It was just too painful for any of them, including Jenna. If their baby boy could not be there with them there was nothing to be thankful for. No Thanksgiving, and no Christmas.

Charlie was a veteran of pain and suffering and the struggle to heal the loss of a child. Charlie decided to risk taking matters into her own hands. She and her group ignored the family's decision, and on December 1st an "Amanda the Panda" volunteer showed up at the family's door with a large box of 24 gifts, one wrapped for each day through Christmas Eve. Charlie described the emotions that went through the home that night as Jenna, whose eyes popped wide open, quickly helped the volunteer spread out the gifts in a line that went through two rooms. Jenna engaged the help of her parents to organize the gifts in order of which would be opened on which day. About thirty days after Christmas, Charlie received a letter from the parents:

"Charlie, thank you so much for what Amanda the Panda did for our family. It was a reality check that the decision we made not to celebrate the holidays because of our son's death was simply the wrong choice."

Charlie told another story about a woman who lost her sweetheart after 60 years of marriage. Amanda the Panda also helped heal that women's broken heart. She e-mailed Charlie at 4 am on December 1st, describing how she couldn't sleep, going through another torturous night of not knowing how to move on. Frustrated to find some healing, she reluctantly had to go open that first gift.

Losing Pamela was the worst day of my life and has been painful so often since. However, if I ever lost one of my three little monkeys, I don't know how I could ever move on and find healing but I guess you do. I think back to that meeting with Terri K and how simple the decision was to start new traditions and not let one holiday go by that the kids and I didn't celebrate who the four of us were now, as a family, and remember that the one seat missing at the table is very special and dear in our hearts forever.

I realized no matter who you have loved and lost, no matter who used to sit in that chair and is now missing, you must always celebrate. It's hard to cut through the pain but if you pause for a moment you will know that the soul that rests in heaven would want you to celebrate. They would tell you:

"It's a holiday, so celebrate!"

....

CHAPTER THIRTY-FOUR

Noah, Why Did You Build That Ark?

"I wish Mommy was still alive to win me more stuffed animals."

Growing up, I had a fish tank for a few years in grade school. I vividly recall the low humming of the filter and bubbles when I was falling asleep at night. That concludes my only pleasant childhood experience with pets.

There was the dog my parents brought home when I was four years old. I don't remember his name because he lasted only a few months. My parents and I have a slightly different recollection of those months, but the one common theme is that dog was a biter. I only remember him having me for a snack a few times. From the first nibble I was terrified of the black, wolf-looking predator with sharp fangs and glow-in-the-dark green eyes, hunting me like a panther. My parents, in their senior years now, seem to recall a tiny black poodle. Regardless of who's right, the compelling similarity is our agreement that the dog was a hunter and I was the hunted.

Like the dog, there is a dark memory over a hamster nightmare. Before I settled on the fish, my parents let me get two hamsters. I guess I thought even if one of them tried to bite me, I could easily manage to get my arm free of its fangs. I enjoyed the hamster experience until somehow one hamster got pregnant out of wedlock and I was punished with about 700 furless babies. Typical of my upbringing, my parents refused to let me dodge my responsibilities as a new hamster step-parent, and I was tasked with learning how to manage and raise this hamster family. There was only one problem. I was one day late getting advice from the local Pet Smart manager. The Pet Doctor gave me one cautious directive, "DO NOT let any humans touch the babies" or the male hamster's instinct, for some reason, is to ahhh, well, let's just say, "*off* them."

My experience with pets in my youth has given me a certain demeanor toward animals. I don't hate them. I just don't want them. It's like that bachelor we all know who doesn't want to settle down, get married, and for sure doesn't want kids. Yet he likes playing with them for a couple hours and usually is a great entertainer, as long as he can give the kids back to their parents when he's tired of playing Candyland.

After Pamela and I were introduced, we had a traditional date. I came to her neighborhood in Philly; we went out for a drink and a few appetizers. We spent hours at a local hole-in-the-wall pub around the corner from her house, then decided to go back to her place and chill out for some TV, conversation, and a few laughs. When we got to the top of the long, narrow stairwell that led to her third-floor apartment, I was stunned by what I heard: barking, meowing, and chirping. She had somehow stuffed three cats, a dog, and a bird in a small Philadelphia walk-up apartment about the size of most mini-vans.

My first introduction was with Pamela's black dog, and I am not kidding when I say it looked exactly like a black wolf. Even my parents will agree to that. I was very unsure about the wolf. On the one hand, it brought back memories of being hunted in the basement by my parent's dog, but this dog's name was "Sweetie." Yeah I know. How the heck could I show fear in front of this hot blond who just offered me a drink at her place with a dog named Sweetie? I didn't have to spend much more time worrying about it, as not one, not two, but three cats surrounded us in the living room. One was a long-haired fur ball with crazy eyes named Kiki, another was an ugly orange cat that never stopped meowing. I don't recall its name, mostly because later that night I asked Pamela to put the damn thing outside. Then a black one that hid under the bookshelf as if ready to strike at the first sign of conflict. If that wasn't enough, guarding the bathroom was this chirping yellow bird bouncing all over the place, thankfully in a cage. I wasn't sure if he was happy to see Pamela and get some birdseed or yelling at me to open the cage door and get him out of there, before the three cats tortured him again.

At that moment I felt like the biblical character, Noah, watching all these animals somehow fit on that great ark that God told me to spend my entire year building. I pictured Noah back then feeling like I did that night, looking at his surroundings, shaking his head, and wondering, "Man, is this really worth it? Should I cut and run, or see where this adventure sails me to?"

You now know that, like Noah, I bit the bullet and took the trip. You remember Noah's journey, but let me tell you about my adventure of chasing love at first sight (you thought I was going to say *bite*, didn't you?). After spending some time at Pamela's petting zoo, the obvious next move was to invite her to my place for a date night.

I shared an apartment with my old college roommate, Charlie. Conveniently, our place was about ten minutes from where Pamela worked. The other benefit of the location was that Charlie's parents lived about twenty minutes away. That made it easy for me to invite Pamela over, let Charlie say a quick hello, then tell him to scram for the night.

The only part of the plan I didn't think through was the wolf. Looking back on it, I should have realized if Pamela was going to spend the night, the dog had to come with her. She had to work the next morning and wouldn't have enough time to drive all the way back in the city, deal with Sweetie, and then drive all the way back out to the suburbs. That caused a slight dilemma that required a few executive decisions and, frankly, some risk taking on my part.

First, ours was a No Dogs Allowed apartment. However, Charlie and I were very friendly with the apartment manager, having gone out a few times with her and her friends. If someone found the dog I figured we could avoid the fine, and our good looks and charm would prevent anyone trying to kick us out, thinking we'd hidden the dog all year in our apartment. But the real risk was that the apartment manager had a crush on me and we'd gone out on a few dates in the recent past. I was already in the dog house, since I'd dropped the hint I wasn't interested shortly before meeting Pamela for the first time. I was more worried about getting kicked by her than getting evicted from the apartment complex. Either way, if something went wrong, good ol' innocent Charlie was going down with me.

Pamela had saved Sweetie from the S.P.C.A. when she moved to Philadelphia. In Pamela-like fashion, she picked Sweetie out among tons of other dogs because she looked most down on her luck, a heavily abused dog on her last legs. This story of Pamela's unconditional love and affection for Sweetie made that dog one of the happiest mutts you'll ever find.

Keeping the dog overnight wasn't that troublesome. Sweetie didn't bark, she let Pamela and me snuggle on the couch without interfering. The next day after Pamela left for work the dog accepted being put on the leash without a hitch. Just when I thought maybe I had started to adopt a soft side for animals, it all went south. As I opened the apartment stairwell door, Sweetie spotted a squirrel running from one of the many trees in our apartment complex, and off she went. I guess growing up in the city it was rare she had to control herself from a squirrel shooting across her line of sight. Our apartment complex wasn't the ideal place for me to take up dog walking, as it was called "The Woods" for only one reason—trees, and hundreds of squirrels, and rabbits everywhere.

Quickly this timid, calm dog turned into the greyhound at the dog races chasing the mechanical rabbit. And she wasn't chasing the squirrel in circles but throughout our three-acre apartment complex of forty identical apartment buildings. My blood pressure was sky high, as was my anxiety meter. My first immediate physical reaction was: *This dog is faster than a jet airplane. I'll never catch her.* Then my emotional distress kicked in: *How the hell will I ever tell Pamela I lost her dog, her four legged soul mate, all in just two hours after being left alone?* I may not be a pet lover, but it didn't take much empathy to realize Pamela's happiness the last few years depended sharply on making Sweetie feel loved.

I quickly started canvassing the apartment complex to find this dog. It was find Sweetie, or lose the love I'd waited more than 25 years to find. I had no time to waste and unfortunately had no shirt on either. I'd figured I was just going to stand in the apartment doorway and let Sweetie pee on a tree, and then back up the stairs. Now I was running around an apartment complex without a shirt, stumbling around people's backyards yelling, "Sweeeeeeeetie, Sweeeeeeetie." That was the moment I really got scared, not that the apartment manager might see me, but what man goes around on a mid-Monday morning walk through strangers' backyards yelling "Sweetie"? At that point my mind, body, and soul were in shambles. I was so frustrated, thinking: *There is no way this darn dog is going to know which apartment building it darted out of.* Finally, I just gave up and started walking back to my place, occasionally—with less volume—moaning, "Sweeetieeee."

As I turned the last corner to the front of my place, there she was. That freakin' dog found her way to my door! One thought pierced my mind: *I hate this blasted dog!*

After we were back in the apartment and I'd bolted the doors and windows, I had to hear Pamela's voice to feel I could put the whole Alcatraz escape behind me. I called her at work, knowing I'd get the obvious opening question:

"How is Sweetie doing?"

I quickly prepared the appropriate response…tell her absolutely nothing!

"She's fine, we're fine. When are you getting off work?"

Several months later in our journey on the Great Ark of Love, Pamela and I agreed to move into a place of our own together. I said goodbye to Charlie and my official life as a bachelor, and Pamela said goodbye to the city streets. Deciding to rent a house meant we were very serious about spending the rest of our lives together. Although we weren't officially engaged, we did have many of the necessary talks to be sure there would be no storms in our Voyage to Eternal Love. We talked about kids, religion, money, and—oh yeah—PETS.

I knew choosing Pamela as the one for me meant I'd forever live with pets. The trick was how I was going to be fair about it, supportive of her love for animals, yet make sure it stayed under control. If she could have so many of Noah's original passengers in that tiny city apartment, I could only imagine how quickly a three-story rental house could convert into a tiny biblical vessel, saving pet after pet throughout the city of Philadelphia. I had to compromise, but control, this one obstacle in our Quest for True Happiness.

I played the perfect angle. I told her I understood we were now a family, and moving in together meant Sweetie was mine, as well. We were a team. However, I was clear that, "As in real life, not everyone makes the team. It's what makes it feel special, a real bond of the soul."

What a bunch of crap I was spewing out. Before she came to that same conclusion, I jumped to the point: "If this is a family/team then, as in basketball (the sport with the least number of players on a team), the roster can only have up to five players on the field at any one time. Simplified; "*This relationship will only work in harmony if there are never more than five of us on the McAteer/Jenks roster.*"

I got an immediate agreement from Pamela, until I explained that she and I were two of the five. Sweetie, I knew, was a package deal. So that got us to three. The next one to make the cut was Kiki. Kiki was lucky to have seniority on her side, being with Pamela for more years than even Sweetie. That gave us only one spot on the roster left to fill. I didn't waste my breath suggesting we could just keep the spot open!

It was a struggle for Pamela to figure out who was going to be cut. Then I dropped a bomb on her. I explained that the roster, or maximum allowable capacity of the team, needed to ALWAYS be five. That meant when we decided to have kids the baby was going to own a roster spot. We hoped we'd be blessed with at least two kids and that would most likely limit us to the four humans and Sweetie. Pamela cringed over the scenario but did understand my compromise, especially because we both were driven to raise a family of our own and knew our focus would need to be on our newborn children, not on raising a house full of farm animals. As I once put it, "The last name is McAteer, not McDonald. The nursery rhyme goes 'Old McDonald Had a Farm, not Old Mr. McAteer.'"

In our first six months living together, Pamela was committed to keeping her promise, never letting her weakness of rescuing animals get in the way of tranquility in our new home and life together. We were an official roster of five, as Kiki and another cat made it on the Ark and traveled the seas of romance. Pamela knew the next few years would bring a ring, a wedding, and—sometime—a baby to our lives. I was totally impressed that she was prepared to let one of the cats go at that time.

Then one day I learned that women, pets, and "acting" all go hand in hand.

It was a hot Saturday morning. We were a bit worn down from the work week and a few bottles of wine the night before. It was too hot to even go for a walk. We both needed some fuel, which meant coffee and some breakfast sandwiches from the local bagel shop. We also had grown bored with the morning's uneventful schedule. As we drove through the busy shopping center looking for a parking spot by the bagel shop, Pamela suggested we go into the pet store to look around. Even in a state of blurry, hangover brain-fog, I came to my wits and said, "Oh no. We are not going in there. No way. Not today. You are so bored, I know the first pet you see you're going to *have to have it*."

I was sleep-deprived and hungry, which equals crankiness for me. I could see the whole weekend crashing within minutes of her begging for a pet, and me steaming that we were having a fighting 'debate' over breaking our cardinal 'five member team' rule.

As she pushed me to consider going into the pet store, Pamela swore to me that would not happen. In a moment of weakness, mesmerized by her blue eyes, her contagious smile, and the cheese dripping down my hand from my breakfast sandwich, I agreed to go in. Although still in a daze, I knew for us as a couple, entering that store was the same as entering The Valley of Relationship Death. As luck would have it, I noticed the pet store didn't have any cats or dogs for sale—huge win for the day. Of course Pamela noticed that, as well, and tried to recommend a longer drive—to the S.P.C.A.

"The only way I will ever step foot in an S.P.C.A. with you is if we were dropping off!"

So she counted her blessings that she simply got me in the pet store, and we cruised the aisles. I actually was having fun looking for some silly dog toys for Sweetie and various gadgets to annoy Kiki with. Then my ears almost dropped off my head as Pamela turned to me and said,

"Kevin, look at the cute bunny. Awwww, he is precious."

I stood there with my half-fake smile saying, "Oh yeah, sure he's cute. Excuse me. Where is this conversation headed?" As you have figured out, she spent the next ten minutes trying to convince me we needed a rabbit. I went from annoyed, to trying to brush my moodiness off with sarcasm, to downright pissed. Pamela, as I'd learned in our first six months of dating, couldn't let go of something if she really, *really* wanted it. That trait rarely was a problem, because she wasn't a person of material things and was the world's greatest discount shopper. However, that day she had her heart set on that long-eared Hasenpfeffer.

I also learned that when Pamela was really driven to have something, she would lose her common-sense muscle. (It is interesting that all the people in the Bible thought the same thing about Noah. Who in his right mind starts building an ark for animals?)

I tried to reason with her. "How in the world are you going to take care of a rabbit when we have almost no backyard and it's a hundred degrees out?"

She may have lost her common sense but she was smart enough to not even suggest we'd keep the rabbit in the house. After she realized I was not going to break on this and my blood pressure was hitting its peak, she let it go. To get our minds off wanting to strangle each other, we agreed to just get our cat and dog each a treat and head home.

We got in the car, I started the engine and, as I reached for the radio buttons to find something to quickly change our mood, I turned to see Pamela in a full-out sobbing fit. I don't mean "get pulled over by the cop and squeeze out a few tears to get out of a ticket" sobbing. I mean trembling tears, streaming down her face like it's Niagara Falls.

I said, "Come on, Pamela, is this really about the rabbit?"

"No, I'm just upset."

At that moment I got a bit scared and wondered what she'd been keeping in so long that was now hitting her like a tidal wave. I pleaded with her to let me in and tell me what had her so shaken. Finally she did fess up. Through a lot more tears, she admitted she had her heart set on the rabbit, and was sure it was not going to be a burden. She'd figured I would understand, and just say "Yes, of course."

Oh, man. I was now all screwed up in the head and heart. I mean, I was upset we were going back to that emotional place where we'd ended in the store, and at the same time she had me hurting for her because she was so down and blue. We just sat there in the car, staring out the front window. I realized this was a moment of truth in our relationship. I'm not sure to this day if it was the tears, my hangover, or how good that sandwich made my stomach feel, but I caved in to a single second of weakness and said, "Okay, if this rabbit has you this upset, then fine, go ahead and get it."

She turned to me, her eyes drowning in tears, her hands full of soaked tissues. "Are you serious?"

"Yes."

Then, as they say in the hood, she flipped her script. Pamela turned from a grieving soul to a happy circus clown so quickly; even *she* knew the jig was up on her fake sadness. And you know what? She could care less. She got her "Yes," then popped out of the car all giddy and skipped into the store to get that rabbit. She ambushed me. I'd been had. I will never witness in my life such despair that in less than a millisecond turns to an overwhelming "gotcha" joy.

Thankfully, she never again attempted that charade. That steamy Saturday morning was the final time I was taken in by such hogwash.

Thanks to Noah and all his animals on the Ark, I now have tons of pet stories. Like the time Kiki got stuck in the tree outside our house and Pamela called 911 to see if they could send someone over to help. I came home to three large fire ladder-trucks, trying to get that stinking fur ball down.

There was our horrible inability to name our pets. We let the kids name the next wave of cats. The first one Kevin Patrick named "Kattie" (pronounced *cat-tea*). When Kattie ran away, Amanda's shot at naming the gray cat we got was: "Gray."

Even in our darkest hours as a family, a few of Pamela's closest girlfriends staying with us agreed to drive her two hours to pick up a starved, flea-infested kitten. That cat lasted only hours after I watched fleas do summersaults in front of my eyes at the dinner table. I reminded her and her partners in crime that the doctors discouraged having cats while her white blood count was at such risky levels.

Oh, but don't worry, the good doctor did team up with her when she was in remission to suggest getting a golden retriever to motivate her to get out and take walks in the neighborhood. I tried reminding the Doc and Pamela we had three little kids at home. She could strengthen her legs chasing them, while I, on the other hand, met the demands of a job that required travel. Not to mention she was still going through bouts of chemo side effects.

"Does anyone think having a dog might be a little more than we can handle?"

Yeah, that fell on deaf ears. Later I found out the good doctor was an owner of two Labs!

Through all this, there was one animal I will remember affectionately. The frog. A frog, that still today is the connection between Pamela and her little baby boy, Christopher. The one difference between the frog and the rest of the pets was that this one is not real. The frog I refer to is the green rubber, wiggly amphibian from the boardwalk game Flop the Frogs. It's a game you might see at an amusement park, where you pay a dollar and they give you three rubber frogs. You fold them onto a metal catapult, take a big swing with a mallet hammer, and "slam" it pops the frog into the air in a shallow pool of water, in hopes it will land on a plastic rotating lily pad. If you're lucky enough to get that rubber rascal to stay on the lily pad, you win a stuffed animal of your choice.

I have two vivid memories of Pamela, Christopher, and the Flopping Frogs. The first is when Christopher got to watch her play the game for the first time at our favorite vacation spot, the boardwalk along the Jersey shore. All the kids were so excited to watch Pamela's smile light up the night, as she slammed that big hammer down and giggled when the frog flew across the sky and splashed into the pond. That night she couldn't wait to show off her Flop the Frog skill to little C.J. (Christopher James). She was holding him in her left arm, secured on her hip, as she prepared to let that frog fly. We all watched in anticipation, not only to see if she would get the frog on the lily pad but how hard Christopher was going to laugh when he saw her smash that hammer down. Well, she took her best shot and laid into that catapult and, as we all watched, that frog flew off like Superman. Everyone followed the frog, except Christopher, who instead of laughing was bawling in hysterics. The SLAM of the hammer had scared him, and I had to walk away with him and hide a hundred yards from the game to calm him down.

As the years went by, C.J. would get over his fear of the loud SLAM and be right by Pamela's side, taking a hammer or whatever else he could get his hands on to make that frog jump into the lily pad pond. I don't know what made Christopher happier: His boyish use of a hammer, the anticipation of possibly winning a stuffed animal, or watching the explosion of joy on Pamela's face playing that game with her little angels?

The other day, while helping Christopher get ready for bed, I was reminded how special those nights were. Christopher had caught me off guard because he and I had not spoken about Pamela in some time. I was picking up a few things in his room as he put on his pajamas, and picked up an unfamiliar stuffed animal, asking if it was his, and if it was did he really still need it? We had been purging some of his more childish toys for bigger boy toys.

He froze me. "Mommy won it for me, Daddy." It would have been more than four years earlier, if she did in fact win it for him. "I wish Mommy was still alive to win me more stuffed animals."

My heart broke, my eyes overfilled. "I know, pal. I know. I wish she could win you more, too."

All I can think now is if I ever ran into Noah I would say to him: "Noah, thank God you followed your heart, not your head, and built that ark."

CHAPTER THIRTY-FIVE

When are Too Many Shoes Just Too Many?

"You don't understand, I have to know right now, what are you wearing?"

Pets might have been my first obstacle to ensure harmony when we moved in together, but it certainly was not the only personal temptation I had to understand about this new love before taking such a permanent step.

As a young teenager, Pamela spent her first working days at a clothing store in the local mall. Over the next ten years, until she retired to be a full-time mommy, she developed her love for matching outfits, found ways to make every customer look and feel great in the clothes she picked out for them, and—of course—made several, well, probably thousands of employee discount purchases herself.

I thought, when I met Pamela, she must live in an apartment with the largest closet you'd ever find. Or maybe the entire apartment would be like walking into a clothing store, with dresses to the right, pants and shirts to the left, and shoes, purses, costume jewelry everywhere you turned. But that was not the case. She lived in an apartment with normal-sized closets, barely larger than you'd find in a small hotel room. Somehow, she found creative ways to fit into her relatively small living space all the outfits she'd bought on triple discount.

Then came the day we agreed to move in together, a nervous but very exciting time. It's a lot of work to move from one apartment to another, but the work is much greater when two people move from their current apartments into a new place for both. We had to do all the work ourselves, but it was worth the effort, knowing we were taking the next step in a life together. But that feeling ended up on shaky ground one early Friday evening.

I'd spent the last eight years of my life living in apartments with many roommates, so I didn't have much more than a few pieces of furniture, a box of kitchenware, my bed, and a reasonable amount of clothes. All of it took only a few afternoons to box up, and a Saturday to load in a U-Haul and dump into our new place.

It was not quite as easy to move Pamela's stuff. Although blessed with a strong work ethic and a caring soul, she was probably the worst planner I've ever met. Boxing my stuff wasn't really that taxing and I was *the man* in this relationship, so I offered to leave work early for a few days and box her stuff up for her while she worked evenings at the mall. She was so happy I'd offered to take care of my new roommate's stuff. I, on the other hand, was blindsided by confusion, frustration, and misery.

The first afternoon, when I called her to ask how many boxes I should pick up on my way to her apartment, she said 9 or 10. I should have made that 109 or 110. I quickly learned Pamela's secret to fitting all those clothes in such a small amount of closet space. When I opened the first door, I thought I was being trampled by a dozen bulls: clothes, shoes, boxes came tumbling down on me. The next closet contained an avalanche of coats, purses, hats, and outfit after outfit. And you don't want to know what was lurking under the bed—a massive amount of women's apparel covering every square inch.

My mood and game plan quickly changed. I went from anal-organized-label it-guy, to how-the-heck-am-I-going-to-get-all-this-stuff-in-one-truck guy, and then quickly turned into where-the-hell-is-the-nearest-bar-to-get-some-beer guy. After catching my breath, collecting my thoughts, I decided to go back into the eye of the storm and, as they say, "get 'er done."

As I started emptying Pamela's main closet onto the bed so I could make sure I knew how high the hill of clothes would be, I came across a startling sight: black, high-heeled shoes. Not surprising on the face of it, as Pamela would typically wear some type of black shoes to work, when we went out, or even if she was just hanging out. What was breathtaking was not one or two, or ten or twenty pairs of black shoes, but an ocean of black shoes, layers upon layers of them stacked on top of each other in this very narrow closet. Of course, as I dug through I'd find the occasional pair of tan or red shoes, but I couldn't believe how many pairs of black shoes there were. Not one pair was in a shoe box. They were just loosely tossed, one on top of another. I stood in the middle of her bedroom, staring to the left at a

10-foot high hill of clothing on her bed, to the right at an insane number of black shoes, in front of me mounds of purses on the floor, behind me an open doorway that led to the fridge and more beer.

After clearing my head, I tackled this insanity with my normal recipe, sarcasm. Although there was clearly no time for organization, I decided "I am going to pull out every pair of shoes and match them up and find out how many pairs of black shoes there are in here." Of course, throughout my adventure I made several quick calls to Pamela at work to tell her how insane she was and how equally crazy I was to be in love with her.

For at least two hours, I dug through shoes, trying to find each one's identical twin. When I was finally finished, the row of shoes went deep in her living room, family room, and down her hallway. I counted twice to ensure I'd computed the correct number, and finally had it totaled: 132 individual black shoes, 66 matching pairs. There were old shoes, some relatively new shoes, some shoes still with tags on them.

I was considering calling a press conference to tell the world, when suddenly it hit me. (No, not the beer, although it seemed to have taken effect sometime earlier.) Pamela was at work and, I would bet my life, wearing some type of black outfit with yes, black shoes, number 133 and number 134. *Before I call the Guinness Book of World Records with this excess of black shoes, I need to be sure I have the right number.*

I called Pamela as she was nearing the end of her late shift. "What are you wearing?"

She tried to shake my call. "I'm closing up the store. I'll be home soon."

"No, no," I said with despair. "You don't understand. I have to know right now, what are you wearing?"

She described her outfit but failed to detail her clothing all the way down to her feet.

Stuttering, I asked about the shoes. Finally, I had my answer: "YES, YES, I WAS RIGHT, NOW I HAVE THEM ALL. EUREKA!" Then I went into a rant, letting her know she had 67 perfectly matched pairs of virtually the same exact footwear. One hundred and thirty-four black shoes.

Pamela quickly ran out of patience with my rant. She wanted to get off the phone and off her feet, after 8 hours of selling to crazy women all night. The conversation ended when she asked me, "Did you get a lot of packing done, before your strange shoe fetish kicked in?"

"Um, no, I didn't pack a dang thing."

In my mind, I'd accomplished something much more challenging, a feat (what a great pun) many men would not dare to take on. Sometimes we guys are so misunderstood!

CHAPTER THIRTY-SIX

Homeland Security Can't Stop New Year's Eve

I'd found my Holy Grail of parental peace and made sure it was one that Homeland Security couldn't tear away from me.

It can be a challenge for single fathers to keep their kids active and interested for a whole weekend without driving themselves a bit nutty. Face it: most single and divorced fathers would be lost if they didn't have an Xbox or a neighborhood McDonald's with one of those giant playgrounds attached. Of course, there are always exceptions to the stereotype.

The best story of a father being creative to keep his kids excited about Daddy time is from my friend, Rich. On his weekend, he'd been doing his best to play the nurturing parent rather than the typical male-provider role. Like many of us, though, he was totally worn out by Sunday morning. Thoughts of Monday morning pressures at the office, combined with children whose batteries lasted longer than the energizer bunny, was a recipe for a dad to bark all day at his kids rather than engage with them and soak up the final moments before the new week started. One particular weekend he came up with a sure fire way to make sure their weekends together ended the way they started. What made Rich's idea genius was that he also found a way to give himself that Sunday morning break, so he didn't go bonkers on the kids in their final visitation hours. Rich discovered the most secretive place that allowed a dad to sit, read his Sunday morning paper from front to back, and quietly sip his needed sixth cup of coffee. All the while his kids safely ran around until they wore themselves out. The tranquil location he found was full of birds that kept their interest for hours. No, they were not at the zoo. These birds were much larger than a zoo could hold. These birds landed at the local international airport! That's right, the airport—where decades ago you could walk all the way to the departure gate without an airplane ticket or strip search. In the good old days, the only place you couldn't go in an airport without a ticket was the cockpit.

Rich was in the presence of the Holy Grail of parental peace. On Sunday mornings he'd grab his son, daughter, and the New York Times and drive to Newark International Airport, one of the largest and busiest airports on the east coast. He'd head to the longest terminal he could find, that housed probably twenty departure gates and a decent coffee shop, so he could grab a cup of joe and begin scanning the front page headlines. Randomly, he'd peek up over the unfolded shield to spot his two kids, who'd run up and down the long terminal hallway until they had no breath left to gasp. Then they'd stare in amazement at the roar of the planes taking off. Between departures they would daydream of someday being one of the lucky maintenance personnel on the ground, throwing bags on the plane and waiving the giant glow sticks in the air. When all the excitement would simmer down, the kids would strike up a conversation with an awaiting passenger. If it was a really lucky Sunday they might even find a few strangers their own age to play with until the boarding call. Eventually the kids' behavior would start to head south, hunger would set in, and with precision timing Rich would be on his last sip and on the back page of his paper. It was now time for his relief pitcher to come in and close out the day. That's when he'd shuffle on down to the airport McDonald's restaurant, which when located in an airport didn't need to have a playground.

What an invaluable secret of sanity he could pass down from generation to generation. That was until Homeland Security put the kibosh on such fatherly freedom. As we all know, today's airport environment is much different than in the good old days.

I was inspired by Rich's tales of Sunday happiness, and grew desperate to find my version of Newark Airport. At the time I learned of Rich's golden nugget, weekends would either be Pamela in the hospital for a week of chemo, or receiving the treatment as an outpatient and requiring hours of rest at home. I hated her staying overnight in the hospital and being away from the children, but it could be just as tough when she was at home trying to recover. I wanted her in the house every day possible, but I also knew that no matter how necessary her rest, the moment she heard a tiny voice she'd find the drive to crawl out of bed, make it downstairs and not lose a moment with her angels of strength.

When she was in the hospital, I'd often take the day shift at the house with the kids and then take turns with Lyn sleeping on the crappy pull-out recliner in Pamela's hospital room. Those days, I could let things go a bit at the house knowing I had a few days to clean up. It was also a little easier not worrying about making too much noise with the kids. I could be pretty creative those afternoons, like breaking out a game of Toilet Paper Tag with the kids, which basically meant unwrapping a case of Charmin's Ultra Soft tissue and running around the house beaming each other in the back of the head. We could waste a good hour or two with Indoor Broom Hockey, until the game always seemed to end with one of the boys taking a fake hockey puck shot right between the... well, I'm sure you can guess the location.

When Pamela would check out of the hospital and return home, Sundays were the hardest times to escape the house long enough to ensure she slept in as late as possible. One Friday afternoon when I brought her home from the hospital, she was beat up physically but also torn up from all the hours she'd missed with the kids that week. That Saturday she acted like pre-cancer Mommy, going all day with the three of them, ignoring any reminders by me "of doctor's orders" or the alarms I'm sure her body was setting off inside her. It was hard not to sit back in awe of her love for the kids. It just didn't seem fair to play Marshall General.

That Sunday morning I had to get her to rest. After Pamela had bullied can-cer around to play with the kids Friday and Saturday, her body would keep her knocked out for most of the morning. I snuck out of bed and got my platoon out of headquarters by o-seven-hundred hours (07:00). With all three kids in the van, it was time to figure out my Newark Airport plan. My first instinct was a trusted sure thing for hours of entertainment. Like a spaceship giving into a gravitational pull I drove to a McDonald's furthest from our home. Every minute counted.

A mile before reaching Ronald's hamburger house, I discovered my Holy Grail. I was headed down Creedmoor Road, hearing the constant verbal attacks of: "Daddy how much longer? I'm really hungry!" when my 15+ years of hotel experience paid off. We came across the Embassy Suites, a hotel I'd driven by a thousand times on the way to the hospital. My creative subconscious awakened. This 15-story hotel not only offered free breakfast to its guests (a fact we'd overcome) but the hotel is well-known for having a wide-open atrium inside where you could sit in a chair on the lobby floor and see every inch of every hallway all the way to the top of the roof. Like Rich's terminal of fame, at the Embassy those little stinkers could run the hallways of the hotel, and even if one or two of them got ahead of me, I'd never lose sight of them.

As we pulled into the parking garage, all three kids were bewildered. Kevin Patrick asked excitedly, "Daddy, are we going to stay overnight at the hotel?"

Christopher of course inquired, "Daddy, are we going swimming? I don't have my bathing suit."

I gave them a simple response although my head was spinning with possibilities: "No, we're going to eat breakfast."

Then our law-abiding citizen, Amanda, stated with concern, "But Daddy we aren't staying at the hotel. Are you sure we're allowed to just go in and eat breakfast?" To set her mind at ease, I reminded her of my long career working and running hotels, that of all the passengers in the van I was the most experienced hotel operator, clearly aware of the services and amenities offered to hotel guests, as well as to those visiting and not staying in the hotel.

However, I was about to do my best imitation of playing dumb and innocent when we entered the hotel. The kids were fired up as we headed to the elevator to take us to the lobby. Their energy was either from the breakfast menu items they guessed would be at their fingertips or the sight of a bell cart Christopher hoped to ride down the garage parking lot. When the elevator opened we entered paradise: a man-made running creek with fish in the lobby and plenty of greenery with open space to people-watch up to 15 stories high. It had the kids' total attention, and shortly the scent of waffles and the clanging of plates drew us into the breakfast area.

To settle them down and get Amanda off my back for breaking some death sentence law against eating for free, I assured them I'd pay for the breakfast if asked. As a joke we tried to come up with a script for what room we were staying in, in case one of the staff members cornered us. But we knew it would backfire, as Christopher just kept repeating our home phone number, and he wasn't even getting that right.

As we made our way through the crowd, I broke the ice by innocently asking a restaurant hostess if we should seat ourselves. The staff jumped all over us, as any good hotel service team would, seeing a poor, overtired father with three little kids in their restaurant—trying to feed them and be careful they didn't burn themselves at the waffle maker, or spill apple juice on an unsuspecting paying guest. In the end, breakfast was awesome—everything they could possibly want, from donuts to omelets. After a good hour of stuffing our faces and people-watching, we decided it would be good for us to kill some more time with a hotel tour Daddy Style. Everyone grabbed a few fists full of Fruit Loops, tossed them in paper cups, and off we went for what I hoped would be at least a 30-minute adventure.

We spent more than an hour riding the glass elevator up and down, taking turns pressing the elevator buttons, checking out how high we could go before getting nervous, staring at the bottom with our faces pressed on the glass. I particularly had fun watching the hung-over couples stumble into the elevator with their pillow-head hair sticking up everywhere, only to be greeted by three enthusiastic elevator assistants: "Good morning, folks! What button can I press for you?"

If Amanda wasn't so damned cute, she probably would have gotten stepped on by a few of the grumpy guys.

We did it all: elevator rides, bell cart races, ice machine speed-emptying, meeting room break-ins, pool room staring, hallway hide-and-go-seek. Not to mention at least two more trips to the Fruit Loop dispenser to make sure we left a trail of colorful cereal circles all over the facility. Just when we thought we were out of new things to do, we ran into the hotel's talking parrot near the front desk.

Ahhhh, my job here was done. After chaperoning the three free-loaders, I found a huge flat-screen TV showing the NFL pre-game shows. I asked the kids, as a return favor for all the fun, to let me watch a little TV in the empty bar area as they continued wandering around the lobby area. It was so peaceful, and they were so happy. Most important, my cell phone had remained silent—which meant Pamela was still resting.

Occasionally Kevin Patrick would stop by my private TV table to check on the latest sports story. As we sat listening to the injury report for the day, something in our peripheral vision caught our attention. We noticed a gold balloon suspended in air, way up in the hotel, almost at the highest floor. After staring a moment at the mystery of gravity we couldn't seem to solve, we put our focus back on the football predictions. Then Kevin Patrick screamed out, "Dad! Look, there's a second balloon and it's black." I told him we must have missed that one because it blended into the ceiling. Now my hotel operations mind took over and I figured out why the balloons were suspended there in the middle of the hotel sky, noticing the clear netting that covered the open air, attached from the 15th floor hallway railing to the opposite side. As I pointed it out to him and explained the many reasons why a hotel puts netting at the top floors, several gold and black balloons darted out over the 15th floor railing. We both reacted like babies at our first birthday party, jumping up and down pointing at the balloons. We yelled for Amanda and Christopher to look up and immediately decided to grab an elevator and investigate.

As the elevator scaled the building we were all mesmerized, staring at the balloons caught in the web of netting, waiting to see what would happen next.

When the elevator door opened, we all dashed out and the mystery was solved. The answer to our balloon riddle was the most exciting thing we'd seen all day: an entire hotel room completely full with balloons. When I say "full," I mean wall to wall and floor to ceiling, with one hotel manager at the entrance losing the battle of pushing the thousands of balloons out of the room and over the railing. I've never forgotten the date because the balloons remind me, it was December 31, 2006— New Year's Eve! The hotel was sponsoring a big New Year's Eve party that night and they were going to suspend thousands of balloons atop the hotel to unleash when the ball dropped at midnight.

If you think that's great, wait until you hear what the manager said next: "Most of the hotel team works later tonight to help with the party, so I don't have anyone to help me get these balloons out of the room and into our nets. Do you guys want to help?"

It's no mystery what the six-, four-, and two-year-old potential volunteers answered. I sat down in the hallway and stared at those three kids in a sea of balloons with the largest smiles I may ever witness. I felt like the best Dad in all of Raleigh. Maybe—for a morning—the coolest Dad in the world.

As in a perfectly written script, my phone started to ring. It was Pamela. I felt like such a cool-cat I decided to have fun with her on the call.

"Where are you guys? How long have you been gone?" She asked.

"We're at the Embassy Suites Hotel," I replied in a nonchalant tone.

"What? What are you doing there? You have the kids with you, right?"

"Of course I have the kids with me. We're helping the staff get ready for the New Year's Eve party tonight."

"What the hell are you talking about? Let me say hi to them."

"Well you can't right now. They're busy working with the hotel manager. But they should be finished in 10-15 minutes." Man, I was having so much fun being elusive.

"Helping the manager? Kevin, they're little. What the heck could they be doing? That's not even one of your company's hotels. I'm so confused. Did you guys get in trouble or something?"

I didn't want to ruin the high I'd reached so I told her about all the events, ending with the balloons and offering underage labor to the hotel team. The kids were wrapping up their assignment, finding the last few hidden balloons behind the guest room furniture. I couldn't wait for her to talk to each of them and hear their excitement. Amanda almost tossed my phone over the rail by accident, not paying attention to which hand she had the balloon in.

Pamela clearly missed being a part of the fun, so I rallied the troops and we headed down the elevator to go home.

I'd found my Newark Airport and made sure it was one that Homeland Security couldn't tear away from me. As if the balloons weren't celebration enough, the icing on the cake was when we got down to the lobby. As the kids skipped past the front desk to the sliding entrance doors, a very well-dressed manager called out, "I hope you enjoyed your stay. Make sure you come back and see us."

Christopher whispered to me, "Daddy can we come back another day? The man said we can."

Kevin Patrick, with a smile of accomplishment on his face, turned to the manager and said, "Thank you so much. We had a great stay and I'll tell my Dad to make sure we stay here again. You have a real nice hotel."

When the coast was clear and we were on the other side of the glass, Amanda looked at me with those piercing, sky-blue eyes and a serious look on her pretty little face: "Daddy, is it okay he thinks we stayed here? Are you going to pay him for breakfast?"

When the clock struck 12:00 on December 31, 2006, I can say with confidence it was one of the best New Year's Eve celebrations we ever shared as a family. The only difference was that our ball dropped at noon that year, not at midnight

....

CHAPTER THIRTY-SEVEN

Who Ate My Car?

"Kevin, you can kiss my ..."

No life is perfect. Even when Pamela and I thought ours was, we quickly realized you have to live with some things being less than perfect or, in other words, broken. Things just break sometimes in life: a window, a toy, and even relationships. It's our resilience and ability to find the best in this imperfect life that makes us who we are. Since Pamela's passing, two things still remain broken but I've found the strength to carry on and make the best of it.

The hardest to mend is my broken heart.

The hardest to forget is my broken van!

It was a Saturday and too hot to do much with the kids. We'd knocked out most of the day with some time at the pool, but were left with the second half of the day to keep busy once C.J. awakened from his nap. We were still living in New Jersey where our house didn't have central air conditioning, so hanging at home to escape the heat wasn't the ideal family adventure. We did what most overwhelmed parents with bored kids do on a Saturday. No, not the movies or bowling. We went to Target for the afternoon.

We overstocked our cart, making a purchase in every department, from the baby section to women's clothing, back-to-school and craft supplies, and of course the popcorn-hotdog café—a must visit when you have three kids in Target all afternoon.

When we finally arrived home we were pretty beat. We'd made it through the second half of the day and bedtime would soon be upon us. As we brought the children in and settled them down in the house, I offered to take over with tubs and bedtime if Mommy wanted to unpack the van. I liked changing roles with Pamela any night I could, because my work hours often kept me from doing tubs and tuck-in during the week. She was happy to trade off. After I'd settled one of them down, I promised to go outside to help with the heavy items.

Pamela typically became a pack-mule-mom, a routine where moms try to carry more bags in their hands and around their shoulders than the strongest hotel bellman could handle. I always wondered why mothers feel they need to overload themselves rather than ask for help, until a mom clued me in: "It's because when you're alone with multiple kids, you know you only have one trip from the trunk to the house before one of them gets hurt or starts misbehaving."

It started getting dark so I knew Pamela's unloading time was limited. I hurried another one of the kids under the covers and headed outside to help. When I got to the bottom of the stairs she said she was all finished, but I noticed the back trunk was still open. That was the final step so I went out and closed the hatch.

Fast forward to the next morning. When I woke up I decided to head out and grab some bagels and coffee for the morning's breakfast. As I approached the van, I pushed the key remote for the driver's side door to open, but the door wouldn't open. It was weird, I could hear the lock making a noise to unlock but the door wouldn't open. Then I looked inside the van. The door lock was broken off. *Damn*, I thought, *don't tell me someone tried to break into our car right in our own driveway.* As I walked around to the passenger door to see if it was damaged, I was startled when a creature jumped to the corner of the window ready to attack me. I peered in the window wondering, *What the hell could be in the van?* I now noticed that the rubber seal around the window was chewed off. Then I saw the creature running back and forth in the van. It was no alien, it was a damn squirrel. Pamela had taken so long to unpack, leaving the back trunk van door wide open, a squirrel had jumped into the huge hatchback looking for some snacks. I circled to the back of the van, flung the hatch open, and braced myself for this saber-toothed squirrel to flee for its life. After a few calm seconds it dashed out of the van, down the driveway, and was gone forever.

The only problem was that several other things were never to be seen again: the rubber seal around the passenger window, the left corner of the dashboard, and—most aggravating—the use of the driver's side lock mechanism. The door would lock but I couldn't unlock the door when I wanted to get into the van. Ugggh! I knew I should have helped with the groceries.

Of course, rather than go for the bagels and coffee I headed upstairs to let Pamela know what she'd done to the car. After she finished laughing hysterically, I brought her out to see how the door lock was going to be such an inconvenience. Being the main driver of the van and having to manage two kids in car seats and one in a booster, her laughter quickly wore off. She did, however, have a brilliant idea. "Let's get it fixed and most likely the car insurance will cover it."

That's when I started laughing hysterically.

"*Who the hell do you think has squirrel insurance on their stupid car? You let the perpetrator in the van, so you call them and explain that a squirrel ate your car and ask for the next step in getting the repairs covered.*"

I gave her the car insurance number.

"*Fine,*" she said stubbornly. "*I don't care. I'll call.*" And she stormed into the house.

I couldn't wait to overhear the conversation. I could already eagerly anticipate the uncontrollable giggling when the conversation started. Well, when Pamela came outside about 10 minutes later, I asked if the insurance company wanted a description of the squirrel for the police report. I was laughing my butt off and poking fun at her. Pamela looked me dead in the eyes with a serious stare. For a second I thought, *No way did she actually get them to cover the car damage.*

Then she dropped her eyes to the floor and through full-blown tears said, "I can't do it. I can't do it. I can't call them. They are going to think I am sooooo stupid."

Needless to say the ball ended up in my court. After taking the van to a car repair shop, hoping to never have to breathe a word to the insurance company, I found out it would cost $352 to replace the chewed-up parts. *No way, I thought, I'm NOT going to call the insurance company.*

Months went by and Pamela did get totally annoyed with not being able to enter the van from the driver's side door. I agreed to get a second opinion on the repairs and yes, again, the estimate was hundreds of dollars. She did finally call the car insurance company. I made her play back the phone conversation word for word and laughed so hard I almost sprained my shoulder. They laughed at her too, and of course did not cover the squirrel damages.

Ten years later we still have this stupid van all chewed up inside. Occasionally, I take it to another car repair shop, and I still get a quote I can't stomach. But there's a positive ending to this story. Every year when the annual car insurance bill would come in, I'd have that one glorious moment when I'd say, "Hey Pamela, here's the car insurance premium for next year. Can you give them a call while I'm at work and check to see if we can add squirrel vandalism coverage?"

Then I sprint out the door to work, before I hear her scream, "Kevin, you can kiss my…" or maybe "Kevin keep it up and you will need husband vandalism coverage!"

I've learned to smile and enjoy life again, living with the disability of a broken heart. In part because I am sure Pamela is getting a giggle each time I pull up to the neighborhood pool and everyone sees this poor guy struggling to open his driver side door. I can almost hear her voice from above whispering to me:

"Hey, Kevin why not call the insurance company? That Geico Ghecko I'm sure will cover it."

CHAPTER THIRTY-EIGHT

Please Don't Let Go of My Hand

"Okay, bye Daddy, luv ya."

It was finally time to be back at work full-time. The three children seemed emotionally stable. Most nights and weekends I exhausted myself planning and organizing the tribe of people who would help me care for them each week, and make sure the house didn't turn into a condemned daycare center. Though I felt I was aging at a rapid pace, we finally had a routine that gave the children enough stability to feel secure in their everyday lives.

Then one Saturday afternoon as Kevin, Amanda, and Christopher flopped around in the pool with some friends, Julie, mother of two of Amanda's girl-pals, threw my world right into the winds of a tornado: "Is Christopher excited about going into pre-school?"

The "*WHAT!*" I shouted internally, echoed through what seemed to be an empty hole between my ears where a parent's brain once lay. I turned to her: "Oh crap, are you kidding me? He goes to school next month? What in the world is pre-school?"

From that day Julie would be my scholastic guardian angel, making sure every school news bulletin was in front of me. She was committed to making sure I didn't miss a school play, parent teacher meeting, or even the book fair. No matter how small the event, Julie ensured I was all over it. She would prove to be a real life saver. At that moment, though, she was the cause of an immediate code red for a father who thought school started with kindergarten. I had no idea how to find out what school Christopher was supposed to attend, and I had to figure it out within five days, before we left for our planned two-week vacation five states away in Philadelphia.

When I stopped hyperventilating and finally could process a few thoughts, a critical reality hit me. My little boy had never been alone in a strange place with strange people for a day. Little C.J. hadn't been left alone for even an hour since his mom had passed away. This poor three-year-old is going to crumble when he hears he has to go alone to a new school in five weeks. No brother or sister to walk in with, no mother to hold his hand, no security blanket to count on. I was in a panic.

Amanda was very young as well, but not a concern for me because I knew she was attending Baileywick Elementary, the same school where Kevin had attended first grade. I wasn't sure what grade level they were going into, but I knew the school had been amazingly compassionate and cooperative when Pamela became sick, making sure the kids got back into a happy routine. I imagined if I walked in and dropped them off in the school office, a teacher would say, "We wondered when you'd show up Mr. McAteer, Don't worry, we'll get Amanda and Kevin to the right grade and classroom."

But what about Christopher? I had no experience picking out schools or teachers. That was one of Pamela's important roles in our marriage.

Since it was the middle of summer, the schools weren't even open for me to drop by for a little investigative sales call. I went through every phone number I could find in my computer and cell phone, even looking in a bunch of old notebooks and phone books in Pamela's purses. I finally collected what appeared to be personal cell phones and email addresses from some teachers we'd communicated with to keep track of the kids' emotional states when Pamela spent weeks in the hospital.

After a few calls and emails I was able to follow the bread crumbs to Ms. Kathy, Amanda's teacher the year before at Good Shepherd Lutheran Church. I thought Amanda had gone to kindergarten there and moved on to 1st grade at Baileywick Elementary. Boy, did I have my head up my you-know-what. Apparently that was the pre-school Amanda attended at Good Shepherd. She was now going into Baileywick as a kindergarten student. *When did pre-school come into the picture?*

In quick fashion I set up a call with Ms. Kathy, who helped me get everything organized. Good Shepherd Lutheran Church was Pamela's mom's church and we'd often gone back and forth from there to the Catholic church, St. Francis. Pamela chose Good Shepherd as Amanda's pre-school because she knew many of the families and faculty there and grandma was active in the church. She was always buzzing around the school and church offices. The teachers were great with the kids and

I was happy I'd found a school for Christopher, especially since it would start six days after our return from vacation. But meeting Ms. Kathy brought on a whole new wave of anxiety.

Ms. Kathy hosted an orientation for the parents and children just days before we were to leave for Philadelphia. A senior teacher and very good at what she does, Ms. Kathy is strict about the rules and gives the impression that even as a parent you'd better toe the line or she'll yank your ear off. Here's what I recall from Ms. Kathy's opening remarks: *"No parents in the classroom or peeking through the window or waiting outside the door. Absolutely every kid must be potty trained before the first day of pre-school or they have to wait another semester before starting."*

Oh great, so now in three weeks I had the following assignments to get my little guy on the right track or risk the beginning of an educational lifetime of disappointment:

Assignment One:
> Get Christopher out of the crib and sleeping in a bed. Unfortunately we'd be sleeping in a different house almost every two days while on vacation.

Assignment Two:
> Get him out of pull-ups and totally potty trained while on planes, trains and automobiles.

Assignment Three:
> Figure out how I was going to instill in him the confidence to let go of my hand and enter into a room full of strangers on his first day of school, without his mom by his side.

Experts suggest a number of behavior-changing tricks to get your youngster out of his crib and out of his pull-ups, but the main advice is do it over several weeks when everything else they do is a normal routine. Well, that wasn't going to happen. We were about to head on our first trip to see all the family and friends who stood by us when Pamela was laid to rest. We had plans to stay with friends in our old neighborhood in New Jersey, and most likely sleep in sleeping bags. Then off to Philadelphia to visit family and friends from my upbringing, then to Wildwood, New Jersey for a week at the shore with aunts, uncles, and cousins the kids had only met once—at Pamela's funeral. I thought I'd go out of my mind. No crib, no diapers, off to pre-school in three weeks, and almost every day in a new place to lay our heads and, more important, find the damn toilet.

Kids are so resilient and adaptable. I don't know if it was luck, parental skill, or a blessing from someone special above, but days from coming home Christopher had stopped peeing his pants and had not slept in a crib for almost five days! I couldn't believe it. I'd always thought of miracles as big events such as crossing the Red Sea or healing a blind man, but I swear both would have seemed easier to me than this miracle of parenthood.

We were back home, I had a lot going on emotionally, and we were three days from the start of school. I worried about how the teachers and Baileywick students would approach Kevin Patrick after he'd lost his mom in the final months of the previous school year. I imagined how wearing it must have felt for Kevin Patrick, a young boy who just wants to blend in, only to be asked dozens of times, "Are you doing okay? How is your Dad doing?"

Then there was Amanda. Although she loves school, she was going into the big two-story elementary school for the first time. She always had looked at her older brother as a source of safety, but Kevin rode the bus to school, and we all know how tough it is for newbies to jump up on that school bus even if your brother is on it. I wondered with such concern how that whole scene was going to play out.

Then there's the innocent little boy who'd spent every one of his 780 days in this world by his Mommy's side until her death on Feb. 17th. Since then, Grandma, Christina, or I had been there for him daily, helping him through his falls, trips, and spills. *Now* I have to pry his fingers from my hand in the middle of a parking lot and let him go? He's three years old—it's just not fair.

D-day arrived. It was time to take Christopher to that first day of school. All I could hear in my numb brain was Ms. Kathy saying to the parents, "I know it's hard to let your little ones go, but let go you will do." She asked us to trust that what would happen on day one would be best for the kids and for the parents: "We will not let you even come in the doors of the school. We will meet you out front, take your children, and embrace them."

C.J. was excited about school. What kid is not fired up about shopping for a new book bag, #2 pencils, notebooks, a Star Wars lunch box, and erasers he'll never use? I think it was for him a feeling of taking the next step into manhood. But as parents we have all witnessed a young child lose control of their emotions as they kick, scream, and hang on to their mothers or fathers for dear life, tons of other students and proud parents watching as the parent tries to peel them away to turn them over to the warden—I mean *teacher*. Oh man, that was a real life movie scene I couldn't pray enough to let us both avoid.

And then there we were, pulling into Good Shepherd's parking lot. Not only was this day one of school but, to add to the emotional stress, Christopher's classroom would be the one closest to the church where his mother's funeral service had been held six months earlier. As we waited a few moments in the car sharing small talk, I couldn't help but get choked up by the view through my front windshield. Dozens of kids gathered in front of the school doors, most with their moms and many with their mother and father. I had a stabbing pain in my gut, thinking how Pamela would have done anything to be the one sitting in this front seat, about to escort her little buddy to his first day of school. It clearly was time to step out of the controlled environment of my car into the open parking lot, for everyone to see if Christopher was going to be able to let go of my hand.

We stood in the background of a growing crowd of parents, mostly because I wanted to avoid being in the spotlight, but also I didn't think I could handle it if someone recognized me and asked, "How are you doing?" or, even worse, if they didn't know about Pamela and asked Christopher, "Oh, where is your mommy?"

The door swung open, out came Ms. Kathy and an army of teachers yelling, "*Welcome to your first day of school. Okay parents it's time for us to take your children.*"

My heart began to race as I watched so many mothers hugging their little ones goodbye. I turned to Christopher, we locked eyes, and I slowly bent down to hug him and wish him a great first day. But before I could get down to his level, to wrap my arms around him and his overstuffed school bag, he stuttered, "Okay, bye Daddy, luv ya."

In less than a second he'd pried himself from my hand and all I could see, through the dust kicked up from his jog to Ms. Kathy, was the blur of his red backpack. I sat there bent at the knees watching his every step, waiting for him to turn around to wave, or to see if I was standing by to protect him if needed. But neither happened. Just like that, he let go of my hand and let go of being a baby boy.

I practically crawled to my car and quickly got in as I watched 20 or 30 moms disperse into their mini-vans and SUVs. I pulled my car to the back of the parking lot and wept for what felt like hours. I cried a rainfall of proud tears for that little boy's strength and courage. And I grieved hard for what Pamela lost out on that day.

Deep down I think I'd hoped Amanda would be too frightened to get on that big scary yellow bus hoping to hear at the last minute, "Daddy can you drive me for the first day of school?" But she wanted to step on to that bus, and she did it!

I think I had hoped Christopher would not let go of my hand that morning, but he did. He wanted to! I was so proud of him, but full of sorrow because his letting go was another sign of letting go of Pamela.

CHAPTER THIRTY-NINE

Finding Love on the YMCA Soccer Field

"Kevin you don't get to choose who you fall in love with. It just happens."

It takes a lot of soul searching and courage to re-enter the dating game. After twelve years of being in love and totally committed to the same woman, dating seemed like a past life. I was struggling with making what I felt could be either a wise life-balancing change that could keep me of sound mind, or one that could end up throwing me way out of whack. I decided to see Terri K at the hospital to gain a clearer perspective on my decision. Seeing Terri was like looking in the mirror, only from the inside out. In the discussion with her about dating, she helped me to vocalize what I already knew, that I needed to go out and feel like a man again. I needed to start the process of figuring out who Kevin now was. The previous ten years of my life I didn't need a separate identity. Being happily married and raising kids almost felt like the five of us were quintuplets. But now, I could no longer be a husband. I missed my best friend. The decision was clear. I knew it was time to "jump in."

I needed to be honest with myself about what exactly I was looking for, and even more importantly, what I was *not* looking for. I needed to date for me, for my sanity, which I knew would help me in every role I played, including being a good father. I didn't want to bring a new "friend" into my kids' lives every month, only to have them wonder where that person disappeared to if we stopped seeing each other. I didn't believe in being overprotective of my kid's feelings, but I didn't want to be irresponsible either.

After much deliberation within my internal social boardroom, I came up with three guiding commandments I would consider before seeing someone for any length of time or introducing the kids to them:

- **Take it Slowly** – It had to be that way because of the little extra time I had due to raising three kids, requiring a babysitter every time I wanted to go out, and insuring that I didn't rush anyone into my kids' lives.
- **Not Complicated** – I wanted to be with someone who is self-sufficient and comfortable with where they are as a person; I have too much to overcome without having to deal with someone else's emotional baggage.
- **Kids' Safety** – Making sure that whomever I run in to, doesn't have unmanageable drama that my kids could end up viewing, feeling, or becoming involved in.

I stayed very true to these core values. Over the next year, I met several women I really liked hanging out with and if one of my three "must-haves" had any sign of being compromised, I quickly cut ties with them. That might sound harsh, but I needed to stay honest with myself and thought it even more important to stay honest with them. One instance of this was a time I had gone out to meet a woman for lunch. Before we had even been served, I mentioned that I wouldn't get married again and my reasons why. She replied with, "Is that the line you use on all the girls on a first date? If so, you might want to re-work it, or maybe use it after the waiter serves the salad."

She was probably right. However, I thought it would work out better if I found someone who was in the same 'place' that I was in; wanting to take it very slowly, not wanting to own someone else's baggage.

I discovered shortly after meeting a few people there needed to be a fourth commandment...

- They had to have kids.

There were times I'd have to stop seeing someone after only a few dates, or the first date, and occasionally even after the first twenty minutes. When you're 40 years old, raising kids, and trying to find someone to share limited time with, I think it's okay for everyone to be totally transparent even if it hurts someone else's feelings. I've heard more than once from women, "You know, I want to be mad at you, but I respect that you were honest with me the first time we met, so I can't say you're wrong for wanting to move in a different direction."

I stayed true to my four commandments, even after I had dated someone for more than six months and our kids had grown to be buddies. When one of those core values was on shaky ground, I had to end the relationship. Until one day on a field, at my four-year-old son's YMCA soccer game.

It was a Thursday afternoon just after work. I had run straight over to meet the kids and babysitter at the YMCA. Christopher was playing for a team called the Plums and it was his third game of the season, a grudge match with the Strawberries. Going to his game after a full busy work day was the best release I could have for myself. Especially, at 4:45 pm in Raleigh on a mid-April afternoon, when we're all sick of the winter temperatures that caused many of us Yankees to relocate to North Carolina in the first place. It really was awesome. A cool breeze, hundreds of kids from three – to eight-years old running around on miniature painted soccer fields, and the YMCA staff somehow making it all look incredibly organized. Parents cheered and mingled about. Coaches mentored and frankly, babysat our star athletes. It brought such a feeling of anticipation for the upcoming t-shirt and flip flop season ahead.

I always get so excited about this outdoor sporting tradition. I even follow a secret routine. The office I work at is about six minutes from the soccer fields and conveniently, just around the corner to our housing development. You might be thinking I'd swing by the house or maybe even use my YMCA membership to change from my work clothes into my 'soccer dad comfort' clothes. But after being in an office all day, I can't wait to get outside and watch my kids run around on that perfectly trimmed green grass. So instead, to save time, I would throw a pair of shorts and flip flops in the back seat of my car in the morning and change while I drove the six-minute commute, with only two stop signs along the way. Yes, pants, shoes, socks come off, then shorts and flip flops appear on my body while I try to steer. (The real trick isn't trying to not swerve in and out of lanes, but rather being more careful not to let a big SUV pull up next to me at the stop sign and think I'm some kind of pervert.) Occasionally, I'm really daring and unbutton my work shirt, take off my undershirt (yes covering my face for a split second as I drive), then toss on a new shirt. Thus, I strip myself of all 'work-daddy' clothing to transform into the Plums' biggest fanatic. I know that isn't a wise routine, but sometimes you just have to throw caution to the wind.

With three little kids connected to several school communities, I learned that news can travel as quickly as a jet flying across the country. When people learn of unexpected circumstances that shake your family, true southern kindness flows through the neighborhood, the church and, most of all, the pre-school and ele- mentary school networks. The acts of caring and kindness move faster than the speed of light. Anytime something would come up with the kids at school, I could always count on a friendly 'heads up' from a PTA mom or a teacher who might have had a McAteer Kid float through their classroom at some point in time. At this time of the year it's common practice for the parents to begin planning how to show appreciation for the commitment teachers put in. One such teacher was Christopher's Ms. Amy. I try my best to stay in the loop with parent/school activ- ities like field trips, even the smaller needs such as more paper towels, extra glue sticks, or other school supply needs. Yet by the time I'm able to get caught up with work, the school event/request deadline has passed and I have to beg someone to take my money so I can feel like a part of those that gave unselfishly.

I'd seen some emails flying around from the parents of Ms. Amy's class about what to get her as a thank-you gift, but it was a busy travel week at work so I never had a chance to get my share of the gift money in anyone's hands.

As I watched the Plums take the Strawberries into a 4-4 tie game, with minutes remaining in the first half, something caught my eye other than C.J. licking Cheeto dust off his fingers from when he was on the bench. What grabbed my attention was a woman at the field across from ours. I pay close attention to the kids when they're playing. You can even find me creating a worn-down grass path as I follow them up and down the field. But that game night, I did let my eyes wander a bit. Especially when trying to ignore the sight of #10 rubbing orange fingers all over the front of his uniform.

The distraction was a woman with long blond hair walking around our soccer field. The closer she got, the more I focused in on her. From far away she looked very fit and I must say, attractive. But she was also wearing big, trendy sunglasses that prevented me from seeing half of her face. As she drew closer, I figured she was headed to the snow cone truck. The North Raleigh YMCA is extra special for what the kids and I call The Red Truck, operated by an old timer, a man with a thick southern accent and a hat made from palm trees. Each game, he pulls his red water ice food truck right up to the fields, stations himself in the middle of the action, and plays attitude-changing New Orleans Cajun jazz music. Both kids and adults can't resist visiting him for one of his 50 different flavors of water ice. Anyway, I turned my attention back to the field, knowing I'd better pay attention in case Cheese Boy scored a goal...and, secretly, I figured I could get an extra peek at the woman when she was in line for water ice. I couldn't help but pretend to gaze in her direction, hoping to catch a good look at her, but surprisingly she appeared to be coming right at me. I thought, *Oh wow, my lucky day,* and then I felt some butterflies. My thoughts quickly switched to, *Uh oh, why is she coming straight up to talk to me?*

She walked up with a great big smile and asked, "Are you Christopher's dad, Kevin?"

I thought *Hell yeahhhhh, I am.* I was so proud at that moment to be that dirty Plums' father.

She introduced herself. "I'm Shayna. I was told Christopher played soccer here and my son Mason, from his class, does too. I'm trying to get all the parents from the kid's class to sign a card for Ms. Amy and I took a chance that I'd see you here today."

I, of course, had to reply with nervous sarcasm. "Wow, I feel so important. Or wait... am I on some list of parents who say they'll help but never do?" I remembered there was also a money request to purchase a gift for Ms. Amy. The requested amount was $15.00 but I only had a $20 on me. "Just take the $20. I'm sure someone else didn't send money in and I can cover their part."

Although I told her it wasn't necessary, she insisted on walking back to her purse to get me my change. That gave me time to talk to C.J., hoping to find out if Mason's mom's name was Shannon? Sharon? Shania? *What the hell did she say it was?*

My eyes followed those black shorts as she headed around our field to where her kids were sitting on a blanket watching Mason's game. When she walked back, I figured I might as well get her name right this time so I could send her a 'thank you' email. Not to mention, I'm always trying to build my list of possible play dates for the kids. I made sure I got her name right as we chatted for a few minutes and I learned her subtle accent was from Iowa, where I'd lived for a few years back in the 90s. We ended our conversation by arranging to get the boys together the following week at the soccer fields. I thought, *Man, this girl is really sweet. I have to meet this family.*

When the game was over I found out Christopher knew Mason and his mom very well, and he wanted to track Mason down before we left the field. Amanda and Kevin had been running around the playground and sand pit at the other side of the fields, so I first had to gather my troops, the chairs, water bottles, blanket, and any other useless things my kids threw on my back like a camel. Then, as we moved from the sidelines of the field to the van, we ran right into Mason and his two sisters, Mia and Maddy. The boys took to each other as if they were life-long friends, and our oldest two realized they'd been in the same class a few years back. The only two who didn't know anyone in the crowd were our middle girls,

Amanda and Mia, but they seemed to warm up to each other after only a few minutes. We soon discovered that Amanda and Mia definitely shared more than being the same age. Their personality traits are quite similar. Before we parted ways, I suggested we have them over to our neighborhood pool sometime. It was one of those brushes with parents you walk away from thinking: *I could be good friends with those people.*

I guess you never know how far $15.00 dollars can take you in life. At the YMCA, it usually only got me two cherry water ice treats and a sticky car.

The next week at the field, I looked around for Shayna, Mason, and the girls, but it seemed we had games on opposite fields. With hundreds of kids it can be hard to locate the right parent from fifty yards away. At one point I thought I'd spotted her, and looked for the rest of her family to verify I'd identified the right Iowa transplant. But as I turned my head back to the game for a minute I lost sight of her. In that split second C.J.'s game against the Bananas went bananas. A mother from the opposing team sprang out onto the field and jumped right up in the face of the Plums' head coach. She was screaming in his grill about her son getting knocked over from the rough play by one of C.J.'s teammates.

I've heard of parental rage at kids' sporting events, but this had to be a first here. Doesn't the C in YMCA stand for Christian? I mean, it's four-year-olds. I call it the Bumble Bee League because all sixteen of the players on the field just buzz around the ball no matter where it goes, including if it's fifteen yards out of bounds. It was really shocking that this woman, not her husband—who, by the way, never got out of his beach chair—sprinted screaming into the middle of the playing field, stopped the game, and gave the coach a lot more than a piece of her mind. What made it even tougher for the coach, was the player that upset her was his own son! The whole scene was so embarrassing that all the parents, both coaches, and, I suspect, even the husband of the crazy woman, were grateful the coach hadn't punched her in the nose. All he did was calmly repeat, "Ma'am, I don't teach them to push. It was an accident. Mam, I'm telling you, I don't teach them that."

That excitement, or terror, ended our McAteer night and scared off any other families from coming near our field. After that, Shayna and I emailed each other as the season was coming to a close. We wanted to get the kids together for a play date before the school year ended, when we knew it would be more difficult to stay in touch.

Later that week, we had a six-kid gathering at my house for a Friday-pizza-happy-hour-play-date. The kids really blended and it was fun to watch the six of them run around for hours, as if they were long-lost cousins. Spending time getting to know Shayna was also really great, both of us sharing a bit of our life history. Conveniently, that same weekend Shayna was hosting a birthday party full of girls for her daughter, Maddy, and invited Amanda over for a sleepover with Mia.

Still today, I shake my head when recalling how the beginning of my relationship with Shayna did not follow my #1 commandment, 'Take it Slowly.' Of course it was hard, because of how giddy I was over her personality, as well as head over heels infatuated with her eyes, her smile, and the rest of her that walked around that soccer field. No doubt my heart was falling like a rock for her, and every minute I spent with her felt special. We shared a lot of laughs, our outlooks on parenting, and advice and personal stories of getting through some of life's serious issues. I honestly can say I often tried to slow things down between us. But when it came to how committed I was to the 'Take it slowly,' commandment, Shayna was just as equally committed to 'When I know what I want, why would I wait?'

That's a hard debate to argue when someone has your heart pounding, head spinning, and has opened up your ability to see yourself in the future for the first time in years.

The moral of this story was summed up during a conversation with my good friend, Bill. He was the only person with whom I shared all the highs and lows of my relationship with Shayna, as we tried to stay true to ourselves and still build a life together. One day, while Bill was listening to my rant of how relationships were different for me compared to other widowers or divorcees, he cut me off: "Kevin, you don't get to choose who you fall in love with. It just happens."

I'd heard him tell me that before and always responded with something like, "I hear you. But in my case, with my commitment to my kids and the loss I endured? I won't find that kind of love again. And before you even say it, trust me, I know. I'm not saying I'll be alone. I plan to always have someone dear to me in my life, but real love, true love, unconditional love? That ability was lost for me in '07' and I'm okay with that."

Bill would smirk and continue his love lecture over a cold beer. "Okay, you can think that. But when it happens it will come up and bite you and it may be by someone you never expected it to be. It's not something you get to choose, especially if it's real love."

There are only a few things I hate in this world. I hate terrorism, I hate the Dallas Cowboys, and I hate it when Bill is right!

It is important to know what your values are and live life true to them. When you believe they're the core of who you want to be, don't waiver from them. However, Bill was right. You don't get to choose who you fall in love with. It could be at the most inopportune time, with the most inopportune person. But if it's true love, forever and always love, staring you in the face with oversized sunglasses, bringing back change for a teacher appreciation gift, then you have only one choice—run away from that "love bug" buzzing around the soccer field about to sting you, or let love take its natural course.

Hmmm, maybe I was true to myself and the core of who I am. All I know is, I'll never take for granted what $15.00 can get you, especially at the YMCA soccer field!

CHAPTER FORTY

You Think Your Memory is Bad

"What did Mommy like to do on the weekends?"

I shared a laugh with my parents the other day as they were looking around the house for their car keys, only to find them still in the ignition. They've become so accustomed to the daily ritual of what they call "senior-itis," their teasing of each other about who is losing their memory faster is almost a symbol of unity in their marriage.

One of my favorite senior forgetful moments was when Pamela's mom looked all over the McAteer campus and throughout her car for her very large white-rimmed sunglasses that she carried on top of her head throughout the entire expedition.

There's another side to teasing our elders who experience absent-minded episodes. That's when your parents catch you only north of forty, walking into a room stop-stare and say, "Damn. Now why did I come in here?" You can hear pride in my parents' cackling as they return the razzing, and strip all dignity from me with the hard-hitting reality that at least they have a valid reason for their memory loss: "I'm 65, what's your excuse?"

Imagine, though, if you couldn't remember where you came from. Imagine spending three years with someone every day of your life and just a few years later not being able to recall what she looked like, what she liked to do for fun, the sound of her voice. No, this is not someone experiencing memory loss from a brain injury. It's a young child who's lost a mother, lost what it felt like to be loved by her, lost all memories of special moments with her, and therefore lost more than memory. The little-girl-lost part of herself.

"Daddy, what did Mommy worry about when she thought about me growing up?" That's what eight-year-old Amanda asked me one day.

My family is all too familiar with another kind of memory loss. Shortly after Pamela passed away, her stepfather Gus was diagnosed with advancing Alzheimer's. Lyn and Gus had moved eight houses down the street from us when Pamela was first diagnosed with leukemia. Gus was much more to Pamela than the title "stepfather" would reflect. He was the man who helped raise her and had a major influence on her life. Being a role model for Pamela meant Gus was just as important to my kids as any of their six grandparents. Known to them as "Pop-Elson" his living right down the street during a time of uncertainty made him a symbol of love, stability, and for them normalcy. Not only was Pop a loving figure in their lives, he was part of their daily routine. The kids saw him almost every day, and talked to him on the phone when calling Grandma Elson every morning after they woke up.

I was so scared at the thought of Gus not knowing who we were. He religiously attended the kids' soccer games, watched football with me and the boys, and joined us for church almost every Sunday. Gus was in his mid-seventies and in pretty good physical health for his age. That meant we needed to be ready for a long, confusing, and unpredictable experience with this disease. It would be devastating to the kids to see his awareness of who they were slowly disappear. I dreaded the day I'd hear one of the kids say, "Pop, it's me. It's me, Christopher."

It wasn't long before Lyn had to make the difficult decision to place Gus in a home, to ensure he had around-the-clock care and his absentmindedness didn't cause him or anyone else serious harm. Having Gus no longer living with Grandma Elson was in its own way another loss for the kids. To my surprise he never forgot who Kevin Patrick, Amanda, and Christopher were. He never lost his connection with any of us, although his disease certainly did play tricks on him. He'd tell me stories of how his old business partners brought the police there the night before, trying to get the code from him to where the money and secret pictures were. He knew they'd try to break into his house so he'd fooled them and hid the loot. These stories would get wilder, as if they were flashbacks to his military service some fifty years earlier. His stories were heartbreaking for me to hear. But I gave thanks that he didn't forget who the kids were to him. Anytime they showed up at his new address, they raised his spirits along with everyone else at the assisted-living home.

His mind was kind to him and to us in this way, but his body was not as kind. It wasn't long before Father Time had taken Pop. I daydream that as his soul was raised, Pamela and a large crowd of others were there waiting for him. I can almost hear Gus's feet shuffling up the driveway to Heaven calling out, "Pammy, how the heck are ya? Hey, where do I get a cup of coffee up here?"

There's a fortunate difference between Gus and Amanda's memory loss. Hers can be rebuilt and developed enough to hold a concrete remembrance of her mom and eventually an emotional file cabinet filled for a lifetime. As with rebuilding a house, though, this doesn't happen without some labor of love.

Amanda was struggling with some typical, age-appropriate ups and downs with her girlfriends at school. She had split with her best friend, and I think the absence of a consoling mother left her floundering a bit. Normally I wouldn't run my finger down the yellow pages for a counselor at the first sign of childhood trouble, but there seemed to be something deeper going on than appeared on the surface. One night when I was away, Amanda inadvertently shared with Shayna that she'd been lying throughout the school year about her mom. For some time when a schoolmate had asked why her grandmother came to have lunch with her or why her mom wasn't on a school trip she'd respond, "My mom couldn't come today".

I had started taking Amanda to a child therapist. Luckily for us we found one who specialized in the McAteer family. Her name was Dee and she'd been the school counselor at Baileywick Elementary when Kevin Patrick and Amanda attended the school, she knew our story well, and I knew how much of a resource she could be for Amanda. Both Dee and Terri K at Rex guided me and helped assure me I was giving the kids the best chance to get through losing their mom in the healthiest possible way. Dee had retired a few years after Pamela died, but her replacement, Dina, helped us reconnect with Dee—who'd decided to come out of retirement to take on a part-time practice.

Amanda is one of the most caring and sweetest girls you could meet. Because of that she has earned the nickname "the pleaser." I think those attributes, along with her painful past, put her in an emotional difficulty. She felt bad about not having a mom, and would tell a white lie so the other person wouldn't feel bad for asking. Then she'd feel horrible, considering herself a liar. This was bound to occur again and again in her life, and added to her depression. Being able to open up with Shayna seemed to help, but Amanda couldn't seem to get over feeling so blue. With Dee and Dina's help, we were able to get to the root of what was keeping Amanda down. It had less to do with a broken friendship and more with thoughts and emotions over a missing mom.

As Dee spent time with Amanda, working through the elementary school playground drama, she uncovered a deeper insecurity. Amanda didn't lie because it was easier than telling a classmate the harsh reality, "My mom died." She fibbed because she didn't want to engage in a conversation about someone she couldn't even remember. She wasn't missing her mom, she had lost who her mom was.

I knew from working with Terri K during the first year without Pamela that hanging on to precious memories was going to be difficult for the kids. Christopher, being the youngest and having had such a short period of time with Pamela, was going to struggle with any recollection of specifics about his mom. Unfortunately, Terri K was right. She was also right that there would be times he'd subconsciously want to reach out for a connection with Mommy and recount memories that weren't actually his, but rather Kevin's or Amanda's. Christopher would place himself in their stories to have a sense of place, because he was too young to remember actual moments of his time with Pamela.

Amanda, only nineteen months older than Christopher, didn't take others' memories for her storybook, she had her own. Unfortunately, they eventually disappeared, too. Driven by love and loyalty, I committed to finding a few ways to ensure I could keep her memory alive.

- **SAVE THE MOVIES** – Within weeks I'd put all our video tapes and home movies on DVDs. I was so afraid of something damaging the tapes and losing those interactions with the kids. As important, those DVD's would be the last treasure of Pamela's live voice.
- **MOTHERS DAY WAS ABOUT THEM NOW** – Months after Pamela was gone, Mother's Day was on the horizon. I worked round the clock to make each of the kids their own personalized photo collage of their time with Pamela, so at any moment they could find on their wall a spark to remind them of who she was. I think the process of completing those picture frames was my most brutal emotional exercise, other than dealing with Pamela's funeral service. The kids were so happy on Mother's Day morning when they came downstairs and saw three large, gift-wrapped frames of dozens of photographic memories of "Me and Mommy." The tears felt fulfilling to me, as a father and as a widower. Although all their rooms have been painted, changed around, and redecorated several times, those frames always find their distinctive place steps from their bed, a never-dying reminder of "Mommy and Me."
- **FIND STORYTELLERS** – Not long after Pamela left us, Lyn and I asked old neighbors, childhood classmates, close relatives, new friends, and

lifelong friends to send their memories to Lyn. We wanted to one day share with the kids this biography of how the world remembered this woman and friend. We set no parameters. They could share a story, a poem, or a page from a scrapbook. We didn't care if the memories seemed sad or silly, were from the last ten years, or when Pamela was ten years old.

These memory-rebuilding steps, however, were not enough. At Amanda's age, I discovered she needed less emotional certainty of who Mommy was and more to grasp onto concrete memories of Pamela. Dee asked Amanda to write down some questions she'd like answers to about her mom.

WHat was shes favorite flower?

W Hatwas her favrite Job?

what did she like to be as holla ween?

what was her favorite singer?

The questions were completely surprising to me, more what I would have expected from a pre-schooler. But that's how difficult it is to get inside a young mind, even if the child is mature beyond their age.

At Dee's suggestion, Amanda and I wrote down all her questions and created a scrapbook of photos, stories, and drawings of her interpretation of their answers.

She would ask such questions as, "What did Mommy like to do on the weekends?"

I would say, "She liked to go garage sale shopping."

Then Amanda would put her mind, artistic ability, and heartfelt love on a page to represent what this looked like in her mind.

I quickly discovered that as an adult I lean more on emotional aspects of memories, I guess you could say spiritual. Amanda needed to know Pamela's favorite color, what food she liked to cook. She had to rebuild these fundamental, concrete memories before she could develop more emotional attachments to Pamela. Some things came easy:

"What was her favorite color?" BAM, "Pink."

"What was her favorite animal?" POW, "Sweetie, her black dog."

As we listed the very basic questions of this elementary school child, I suddenly realized that many concrete memories had disappeared from my memory:

"What was her favorite food to eat?" "Ahh, well, no wait, um, I think pasta?"

More questions kept coming, and fewer answers. That's when I realized we'd stumbled onto a fabulous project that would represent a missing mother's love. Many of these questions were for Lyn to answer, or for Amanda to call or email Art, or even to compare their answers with what Uncle Chris might say. Here was an opportunity for Amanda, five years after her mom's death, to offer her closest loved ones a concrete way to help us adults rebuild our memories of Pamela. This gift would also help her brothers, and maybe one day her children.

This little girl who'd been aching for truth and facts was now an energetic and motivated investigator, embracing the most important autobiography project in McAteer elementary history.

I know as I get older I'll continue to forget where I put my car keys, or where I last left the remote control. Sometimes I wish I could erase the sad memories of Gus experiencing Alzheimer's. There are days the children's hurt over losing Pamela can't be ignored. Those days it helps to remember just when a child's memory seems lost forever you can rebuild it, one priceless brick at a time.

It's Okay to Get Caught in the Women's Underwear Aisle

"Babe, you're not going to believe what happened to me today in the woman's underwear section at Marshalls."

It was Thursday afternoon; I had gotten out early from a lunch meeting that was being held by a local marketing organization. Driving to my office across town I thought, *It's such a nice day out I could really use a little "me" time.* As I waited at the traffic light, feeling the cool air blowing in my window, I noticed a shopping center. *Why not go do some random, mindless shopping?* A feeling of such freedom came over me, as well as a bit of mischievousness. It was like playing hooky from high school (not that I know what that feels like…).

I decided to go into one of the larger retail stores. It was liberating to walk around inside without any to-do list, any real necessities to shop for, and for once, not feeling as if I were racing a clock. I simply floated about the store.

First, I swung by the sportswear aisle and then, briefly, over to look at the ties. As I stepped past the luggage area, out of the corner of my eye I noticed the women's underwear section, located near the store's display of socks. *Maybe I'll check out something sexy for my girlfriend*, I thought to myself. That whole scene can sometimes be uncomfortable for men, but it was about 1:00 pm, in the middle of a work and school day. *No one will even notice me there,* I reassured myself, anxiously huddling by the socks. When the coast seemed clear and I was just about to make my move into 'Fantasy Land,' out of nowhere a woman in her mid-forties approached. She stopped me dead in my tracks, and with a megaphone-like voice asked, "Is your name Kevin?"

Suddenly the temperature in the store seemed to hit the roof and I felt my face turn all sorts of colors. I uncomfortably stuttered back, "Uh..., yes." In seconds I went through my mental Rolodex of contacts and acquaintances wondering; *Does she recognize me from work? No, don't tell me... Hhmm...she knows me from the kids' school?*

Thankfully, she immediately explained, "I saw the article about you and your family."

I was still feeling numb, but now for a different reason. Article? What article is this person referring to? And why is she spying on me in the women's underwear section? Wait a minute... Yes, she has the wrong guy! Oh crap, but she knew my name?

She cleared up the confusion. "I saw the article published in the local *News & Observer* online. I read about how you and your family dealt with cancer, and I wanted you to know the article really helped me to have hope and confidence that my family can get through cancer as well. My husband was recently diagnosed and is in the middle of his treatment at Rex Hospital. We have a couple of young kids at home and your story both inspired me, and helped educate me, on how to cope with everything." She paused before adding, "I am so sorry about your wife."

I have never felt comfortable responding to that comment of sympathy, even when I know the person is being sincere. I simply responded with my usual, "Oh, thanks," and followed up by asking how her husband was doing and the outlook of his treatment.

"So far they think he'll get through it. My husband is strong. But before I read about you and your children, I didn't know how I was going to get through it all."

I told her I would keep their family in my prayers and honestly at that very moment I selfishly started to ask God to help me find a way out of the underwear section. I casually stepped away, trying to politely break the conversation that was holding me hostage. I grabbed a few pairs of socks off the display and felt my eyes start to fill up. I knew I needed to make my way towards the checkout counter and get out of the store before my emotions overtook me.

As I walked outside the sun shone in my eyes and I squinted back a few tears, feeling as if I'd just dodged a serious accident. You know. That intense relief that floods over you, telling you it's okay and you've escaped danger. You might take a deep breath, and then realize your heart's still racing and you're unable to recapture that calm feeling you had before the danger approached. As I crossed the parking lot to my car, I did some speedy soul searching. *I really need to pray for others more consistently. Maybe today was a wakeup call to not be so casual about forgetting to pray. Today I'll add to the prayer list, uh, oh… Please don't tell me I forgot her name already?*

Standing in front of my car, I drifted away into a maze of emotions, one being an overwhelming feeling of self-pride. I realized, *I really did good letting Bonnie write our story. Wow, it's been three years since it was written and that woman still found it and was touched in such a deep manner.* At the same time, I was bewildered by the crazy coincidences of this whole scene.

- What if I hadn't been invited to that lunch meeting? I would have never been in that area.
- What if the meeting had ended on time? I would have had to head directly back to the office.
- Wait a minute, I also never shop at that department store.
- What drove me to go into that store? If I didn't take the risk of stepping toward the ladies underwear section, she would have never met me. Not today, probably not ever.

Everyone has those "It must be destiny" moments, where you meet someone, at some place, at some time that could never have happened if one tiny circumstance was different.

- Maybe it was destiny that I had chosen to participate in the article.
- Maybe that's why, when I felt so wrong about working on it with Bonnie, I pushed my feelings down and forced myself to open up to her.
- Maybe this was a small part to the answer "why" Pamela had to leave life so early.
- Maybe Pamela's story had to be written so it could help this one family persevere through their own life-changing challenge.

As if I were standing in a deep pool of quicksand, I suddenly felt a heavy weight of sorrow, reflecting on that time in our lives. I knew what it was like to live the way the woman in the department store was living right now. It's terrible for your spouse who's at risk, in pain, and your innocent children having to go through such confusion and uncertainty. Additionally, there is the overwhelming exhaustion from the stress, hurt, and responsibility you're burdened with to keep it all together.

As I sat in my car, I had a flashback of that walk up our driveway, picking up the Sunday morning *News & Observer* and seeing that picture of Christopher in my arms. I pulled myself together, started my car and wondered how Shayna would react when I said to her, "You're not going to believe what happened to me today in the women's underwear section at Marshalls. Oh, and here are some socks I bought you; I hope they're your size."

Well, one thing good came from that day. It made me feel as though I hadn't aged since the N&O published my ugly mug three years earlier. We all know how critical that is for the 40 and Over Club.

(If you're wondering if I've been back to Marshalls since then, the answer is yes. Although, not at that particular store location, and definitely not without Shayna by my side. I'd rather she be with me to avoid any more embarrassing moments and I'm sure she'd prefer this young-looking stud she's in love with not be alone in the women's underwear section again.)

Months later, I kept thinking back to that day in Marshalls, about Mary, or Linda, or was her name Susan? How did she have the courage to walk up to a perfect stranger in the women's underwear section? What if she was wrong and I wasn't the man she thought she recognized from a three-year-old article? How brave, yet maybe desperate she must have been. Makes me wish I knew how her husband ended up. I wondered when she left the store if she shared our encounter with her kids or her husband? Maybe one day I'll find out that she wrote a story about our encounter that day.

Hmm... I wonder what she would title that story?

Rumpelstiltskin

*I travel for a living and it's our way of staying
connected so they aren't as sad while I'm gone.*

Rumpelstiltskin McAteer stands about three inches tall and, although his stature is small, you quickly notice two things: his fire engine red, spiky hair that makes up a third of his height and, if you're around him enough, his annoying yet catchy cry, "Bah, Bah-Ba, Ba-Ba-Ba-Ba-Bah," closing with the spirited scream, "Rummmmpelstiltskin!"

Rumpel, as we've nicknamed him, has a distinctive place in our McAteer family movie reel, although he was not always well liked in our home. Christopher found him at the bottom of his fast food Happy Meal box one Saturday afternoon. Although I can't recall what animated movie Rumpel's character is from, his look is definitely distinctive. If you're from my generation and a fan of Christmas, you might compare his likeness to the Heat Miser in *The Year Without a Santa Claus* movie. The difference being, when the Christmas movie appears on your TV guide, you wait in anticipation hoping you won't miss it. But in the Rumpel-Happy-Meal case, once Christopher finished shoving handfuls of salty fries in his mouth, he accidently discovered if you tap Rumpel's feet he'll chant the annoying "Bah, Bah-Ba, Ba-Ba-Ba-Ba-Bah." Then, when you're ready to blow a parental gasket, Rumpel sings out his name with such enthusiasm it would make every six-year-old boy grin like the Grinch stealing a child's Christmas toy.

It didn't take long for Christopher to lose ownership of his new friend. I confiscated it from his ketchup-covered hand after the second or third final, final warning, requesting that he stop making that irritating, obnoxious noise while I was driving a van full of kids to our house.

But Rumpel's spell took me over and the forty-three-year-old little boy inside me came out. It was later that night, when Shayna and I were involved in a conversation that progressed from a mature discussion into a debate. Not a mature debate, but rather one that spun way out of control and ended with both of us sarcastically roasting each other about how we'd handle getting kids to clean up after themselves. Just as I could sense my nagging jabs at her were beginning to go too far, I saw something red out of the corner of my eyes. On the bedroom floor, Rumpel was peeking out of the gym bag I'd forgotten to empty after the kids and I returned that afternoon from flag football. .

Shayna had come back into the room to give me what I think might have been her last comment to me regarding her impatience with kids not listening to behavior warnings, I childishly interrupted her with, "Bah, Bah-Ba, Ba-Ba-Ba-Ba-Bah!" Not surprisingly, I received a glare in response. I'm not sure if it was Rumpel's never-ending sound, my wise-ass smirk, or my immature mocking of what was probably a well thought out argumentative point from her side; but either way, the frenzy it sent her into was immensely amusing.

Then came the best part, the moment I knew would change our relationship forever. The seventh or eighth time I pushed the feet of the tall, red plastic haired toy and he screamed, "Rummmmpelstiltskin!"

That's when Shayna launched across the bedroom yelling, "Give me that damn thing! Give it to me now!" Of course, I ran like a school girl being chased by a scary Rottweiler and locked myself in the bathroom. Knowing inside that she'd end her attack if I shut down my jackass behavior, I hid Rumpel and exited my safe haven.

She immediately asked for Rumpel and I refused to turn him over. She responded by searching me like a TSA agent scanning passengers through airport security, regardless of my assuring her he wouldn't be coming back out tonight.

Shayna, of course, threatened to not to give up her search until he was captured.

We spent the next week hiding and finding Rumpel, back and forth between the two of us. The thrill of busting him out to 'burn' the other person while they were involved in a serious conversation was so much fun! The most classic moment was me pranking Shayna by Rumpel when I knew she'd be answering the phones at work. I still chuckle when I think of her, all serious, answering the phone:

"Doctors office, this is Shayna. How may I help you?"

"Bah."

"I'm sorry?" She questioned.

"Bah-Ba."

"Hello?" She asked again.

"Ba-Ba-Ba-Ba-Bah."

"Excuse me, sir? I'm sorry, I can't hear you clearly." She said, but I knew she was now irritatingly playing along.

"Rummmmpelstiltskin!" I played back as a response to her questioning, and hung up.

As I'm sure you can guess, eventually this practical joke of ours grew old. Shayna had gotten much better at hiding Rumpel, and it had been weeks since either of us had exercised our adult right to annoy the other. Then one morning, I was packing for a multiple-day work trip. I can't recall what it was that I was looking for, but I needed something that wasn't on my typical 'to-pack' list. As I searched through some drawers in the dining room for whatever it was, there, lying calmly in the china cabinet drawer amongst a few old candles was Rumple. It felt like finding a hundred dollar bill. You're excited, but then disappointed knowing you have to return it. You look around and wonder, *What if no one claims the money? Basically it's yours, right?* With this rationale, just like a Navy SEAL I captured Rumpel, securing him in my clothing and secretly relocated him into my luggage. Soon after, I said goodbye to the kids and Shayna, and pulling Rumpel out of my luggage, placed him prominently in my laptop bag, making sure I wouldn't forget he was traveling with me.

When I arrived at the airport I went through the usual routine of air travel, double checking to ensure I had my ticket and driver's license handy. Once that was done, I had a moment to relax. I reflected back about my life, my kids and those I love. Especially those I just kissed goodbye. I tried to entertain myself by walking around the terminal since I was ahead of schedule. I wondered, *What am I going to do with Rumpel?* That's when my creative juices kicked in! I proceeded to take pictures of him to send to Shayna's cell phone. Remember, she thought he was still snug in his china cabinet drawer.

First, I took Rumpel to a gate where there weren't any planes departing and held him up on top of the check-in counter. He was positioned just right, with the airport sign glaring smugly over his shoulder. I snapped the photo, then the current state of travel and security reminded me that at any moment the police could tackle me for this, possibly search and interrogate me too. But, as I looked around and saw there wasn't any reaction from the few strangers looking on, I sent the picture via text to Shayna with the subject line of, 'Are you checking in, Sir?'

Her response took only seconds to come in over my phone, a long, but obviously amused rant. I'm not sure what got under her skin more—that I'd found him, or that she had zero shot at getting him back because I'd be in Pittsburgh for four days.

My entertaining torment continued as I took pictures of Rumpel; with a cup of coffee from Starbucks, sitting at a restaurant having lunch with me, and reading a magazine next to me on the plane.

After my flight, as I walked through the Pittsburgh airport, a great idea was accidentally born. I came across a life-size replica of a famous Pittsburgh Steeler, Franco Harris. I'd seen it a dozen times before on trips and had always meant to tell my son about it after I'd returned home, but instead, would wind up forgetting once I walked through the door. Well, not today. Today Rumpel was going to be photographed sitting on Franco's shoulder, like he was going in for a game-winning tackle. I then sent the pic off to Shayna and wrote, "Make sure you show this to Kevin Patrick. Tell him I took Rumpel to the Pittsburgh Steelers' game and we got to meet a famous football player!"

From there the fun just went on, finding experiences on my trip that would be of interest to the little hearts I'd left at home. At breakfast the following day, I sent a pic of Rumpel in a bowl of Fruit Loops cereal, since this was becoming Christopher's main source of daily energy. I also took photos of Rumpel outdoors in the Pittsburgh snow, walking along the sidewalk. Another morning I even got one of him on a treadmill in the hotel's exercise room. The kids loved receiving email pictures of Rumpel getting in a quick jog before they had to head off to catch the bus. My Rumpel saga with Shayna had developed past our practical joking, into a really cool bonding moment for me and the kids during times I couldn't be nearby to hug and kiss them.

On my return trip home, there was a short delay with my last connecting flight. I was innocently filling up Shayna's mobile phone with more pictures of Rumpel to show the kids, hoping to get them excited about my return. After snapping a photo of him near the food court area, next to a big bottle of Heinz Ketchup (the kids and Shayna's favorite vegetable food), I walked by a souvenir store where I saw a huge Hello Kitty stuffed animal. Amanda had moved out of the Hello Kitty stage many months earlier, but I wanted something "girly" to send her. I decided to go into the store to take the picture, but felt awkward about it. Grown women were hovering around the display area I wanted to use in my picture, and I was eyed up by the salesperson behind the cash register. I was about to exit the store and skip the photo shoot when a daredevil feeling took over me. *Awe, it's for Amanda. Go for it,* I told myself. Then, with determination and, honestly, a bit of anxiety, I placed

Rumpel in front of the four-foot tall Hello Kitty and quickly snapped the picture.

I grabbed my little buddy and turned to escape, only to find a woman in my way who had caught the whole photo shoot. She stopped me dead in my tracks and asked, "What are you doing?"

I felt like a guilty driver being pulled over by a policeman for speeding. In those situations, you try to think up a million excuses to tell the officer, trying not to feel like a jailbird. Well, this time I didn't have a canned response to get me out of a 'ticket.' I stuttered back, "Um, well, it's a picture for my daughter. She uh… loves Hello Kitty."

The women was like the cop who sees right through your garbage excuse and says, "Oh, okay. But what's with the little cartoon figure in your hand?"

I'd been busted.

I came clean. Well, somewhat that is. "Rumpel is a toy from one of my kids' Happy Meals. I travel for a living, so I take pictures of it with things I see during my trips that I think might be funny or cool to them. It's our way of staying connected so they aren't so sad while I'm gone."

"That's beautiful!' she exclaimed with a glowing, grandmother-like smile. Her two words hit me, right at the depth of my heart.

"Thanks. Yeah, it is kind of fun." I almost floated on air as I walked out, in a daze of happiness and fulfillment. Not only did her words erase all my anxiety, but they also filled me with fatherly pride.

As I traveled back home on that day's final flight, I gazed out the tiny window, thinking back to that moment in the Hello Kitty store, and found that for the first time while flying home and thinking of my kids I didn't tear up. I found myself having these prophet-like thoughts about being a proud father and how glad I was Ronald McDonald created the Happy Meal.

Happy Meals… Think about all the mystery and power in that simple idea. I often wonder how many moms and dads have found their most effective, behavior-influencing parenting technique in a single, common motivational phrase like, "Christopher, if you're good, I'll take you out for a Happy Meal!"

I was pleased with myself with having started this new tradition. Making memories for the four of us, no, the five of us, without even being in the same zip code.

As someone special once said to me, "That's beautiful."

....

There Aren't Many Good Surprises Left in Life

The once agreeable audience now began to stare in bewilderment.

When we were kids and someone said, "I have a surprise for you," it seemed second nature to be excited about the unknown. As we get older, the positive impact of true surprises seems to fade away and often is replaced with being surprised and thankful when something bad didn't happen to us or a loved one. As a father now in my forties, talking about surprises with others my age or older rarely matches the excited anticipation I used to feel. Now, the surprises I typically hear about are of someone's sudden illness or of somebody losing their job.

During my marriage to Pamela, shortly after I turned 30, I experienced one of the last great fun-filled surprises left for married adults. It sounded something like this: "I'm pregnant."

Oh, Yeah. There's nothing like the anticipation for a husband and wife when finding out you'll be blessed with the miracle of becoming first-time parents.

One night, Pamela and I sat on the couch discussing whether we wanted to know if it would be a girl or a boy. We both had the same desire, to wait until that great day our baby would be born to find out. Pamela, I think, liked the idea because she was always so childlike in her ability to just sit back and smell the roses. I, on the other hand, came to the same conclusion with a little more due diligence and reflection. I subscribed to the theory that, as adults, surprises were no longer what they once were as when we were children. They are instead redefined as unexpected and shocking unfortunate events. I mean, just look at the definition of *surprise*:

sur·prise/sə(r)ˈprīz/
> Verb: (of something unexpected) Cause (someone) to feel mild astonishment or shock.
> Noun: An unexpected or astonishing event, fact, or thing.

Where is the word *fun* in that definition? I was certain that there were no surprises left in life that were going to have a good outcome. Anything that we would label a good experience most likely was pretty predictable and not a true unexpected surprise. Think about where I was in my life at that time. In the years leading up to our first pregnancy (*don't you women love it when men use the term "our" pregnancy or "we're" pregnant!*), I found the love of my life, she agreed to date me, I popped the question, and she actually said yes! That pretty much wraps up all of love's great to-do's. I had a good job with Marriott, a long-lasting, stable company, and was sure to get a raise or a promotion from time to time, but how many times is that really unexpected?

I figured all surprises that could be left for me were one of those worrisome late-night phone calls, like the ones that freaked out my mom when I was younger. She would assume all late calls were from the police station, calling to tell her one of her sons had been locked up. Man, the only surprises I thought could be left in my future were Death, Divorce, &/or Demotion. So after concluding this, I insisted to Pamela that no matter what anyone said, we were going to stand strong and experience one of the last great surprises left for us. We would wait for the day she would deliver our baby, to find out whether it was a boy or girl. We would live in the moment of astonishment during this miraculous event!

Throughout the next several years, we went through life with the same fever of not letting life's routine and mundane realities steal our last few winning "Lotto ticket moments." We didn't cave into the pressure of grandparents trying to convince us they needed to know the sex of the baby so they'd be able to stock up on all the right clothing and baby merchandise. This was especially difficult for us, as our kids were blessed to have three sets of grandparents, all head over heels thrilled that we were adding grandkids to the family tree.

It was such an incredible thrill to be in the delivery room! Each time being full of anxiety and anticipation as one of our kids were born. Hearing those awesome words, "It's a boy" or "It's a girl!" Over the last few years, dozens of co-workers have announced they were having their first baby and the first question I'd ask each time was, "Are you going to find out the baby's sex ahead of time or take the ride of one of life's last great surprises?"

I have not yet heard one couple jump on this thrill ride. It's always been the same answer; "Well, we talked about it, but we really want to figure out how to decorate the room before the baby comes and it'll be so busy after they're born," or, "We were going to wait to find out, but my wife's mom/sister wants to have a big baby shower for her and it's hard to celebrate if you don't know what you're having." Really? How predictable. People can get really boring once they put a ring on their finger and dive into that wedding cake.

At 43 years old I was granted the pleasure of being reminded just how much fun surprises can be. I was in Toronto having a conversation with someone who works at one of our hotels. He was dropping me off for a flight home and telling me what it was like for him and his wife to be having a baby for the first time. I, of course, took full advantage to preach to him, but to no avail. After I boarded my plane, the pilot announced over the loudspeaker, before take-off, that the couple sitting in row 28 were together for the first time in two years since they'd both been deployed by the military overseas.

"On top of thanking them for their service," the pilot continued, "let's please congratulate them on their engagement this weekend!"

Of course all of us roared with applause. Once the clapping calmed down, in typical Southwest Airlines fashion, the pilot brought us back to a loud cheer with his next announcement: "What makes this weekend even more special is that it's their wedding day tomorrow!"

The couple was on leave, got engaged, and must have figured life is so unexpected, especially being in the military, they decided to get married right away. God bless them.

The whole moment really touched me. I stared out that window of reflection once again, counting my life's blessings. The chat in the car with my young co-worker expecting a baby, and being part of another couple embracing one of life's great moments was emotionally overwhelming. I began to tear up, thinking of my kids, Pamela, my family, and how blessed I was to now find love with Shayna when I thought that ability had slipped away from me for a lifetime.

I then realized falling in love with Shayna had given me one more opportunity to live in the moment and feel the thrill of a great surprise. No, not pregnancy. Shayna and I already have six kids within six years of each other. Plus, after Christopher was born, Pamela and I rationalized how blessed we had been as baby makers already, and I had opted to disassemble our machine. Yes, I had my you-know-what, you-know-where 'disassembled.'

So, not a baby surprise this time, but instead a marriage proposal surprise. Yes, I was going to make sure that no matter when I popped the question, it would be an unexpected, unpredictable, and unbelievable surprise that Shayna would never forget.

"But how?" you might ask.

A nightmare traveling experience led me to the answer. I was heading home from a trip to Minnesota a week later and once again flying on Southwest Airlines. I experienced one weather-related flight issue after another. First, my 2:30 p.m. departure from Minnesota turned into a 4:45 p.m., then a 9:00 p.m., and then a, "Sir we will not be flying to Raleigh tonight." The airline offered me two choices; stay overnight in Minnesota and take an early morning flight out with multiple connections, arriving in Raleigh the next afternoon; or leave on a plane in 15 minutes to Chicago, stay overnight there, and take a connecting flight through Philadelphia, arriving in Raleigh at 11:30 a.m.. I took the offer behind 'door number two,' which would get me home earlier the next morning.

I successfully arrived in Chicago late that night and sought out a nearby hotel. Grateful to have caught about four hours of sleep, I managed to drag my over-exhausted numb self back into O'Hare International for my first scheduled flight departing at 8:10 a.m. Then more weather challenges came—a storm about to hit Philadelphia where I was to connect. The Southwest team found a way to reschedule everyone whose final destination was Philly onto a different plane. The hope was that the flight would beat the storm and land in the 'City of Brotherly Love' as their passengers had planned. Those of us heading to Raleigh were asked to hang out for a while and possibly take a direct flight home instead. Without having to fly into Philly, my plane would have me home in Raleigh even earlier—9:30 am!

Wow, I thought to myself, *my luck must be changing*! The ladies at the Southwest counter continued to make announcements, advising all the Philly passengers of their new departure gate, and as they all dispersed I began sensing there might be a problem with my itinerary. Looking around, I noticed nobody else at the Raleigh departure gate but me. *Uh Oh, I wasn't even supposed to be in Chicago. Maybe the airline mixed up my info and hasn't figured out I'm here yet?* Reading my nervousness, the Southwest team at the gate assured me I was on the Raleigh flight. Kindly, they explained the lack of passengers was due to the change in the original flight. Now that the Philly portion of the flight had been rerouted, only a few people remained heading for Raleigh.

Well they were right—"only a few people" were aboard that plane. In all, there were two pilots, three female flight attendants, and one passenger. Who was the passenger, you ask? Yep, Yours Truly! Inside the massive 137-passenger airplane, 136 of the seats remaining empty gave me an eerie feeling. Not knowing where to sit, I went back to row six and buckled myself in. Within seconds the pilot looked out from the cockpit and said, "Hey Kevin, why not move up to the front row? That way I won't have to yell so loud when I give you the announcements."

Getting a kick out of me being their sole passenger, the three flight attendants joined in the amusement and argued over who would get to ask if I'd like a beverage or peanuts to snack on. Southwest, in case you're not aware, is recognized as one of the best customer service companies in the United States. Not only do they do everything they possibly can to accommodate travelers, they do it at one of the best flight rates you can find these days. They also will shock you with humor from time to time, which isn't normally expected from such an important line of work as flying people's loved ones from city to city. Additionally, Southwest has also been known to personalize flights when possible, like the one I experienced with the engaged military couple a few weeks earlier.

After take-off, the flight attendants apparently didn't have much to do other than talk to me for the remaining two hours. And oh, how they could talk! *So much for the dozing I'd been looking forward to since my brief four-hour nap.* But then flight attendant Jill approached, breaking my internal annoyance, and said, "Hey, it's a stocked bar. What do you want? It's all yours!" Unable to resist, I ordered a Bloody Mary and warmed up to the idea of conversing.

As Jill and I talked and she got to know me better, she was moved by the story of Shayna and me. Then, without shyness she blurted out, "When the hell are you going to marry this special woman and make it official?" I answered back that an engagement was definitely in our plans. The last hour of my flight was spent discussing with the three flight attendants how I should "pop the question."

It seemed obvious what the foundation of the engagement plan should be; it should take place on a Southwest flight. If you think about it, fate had to have been leading me to that location. A week earlier, I'd been touched by a couple's engagement on one of their flights, then went from a nightmare flying expedition to being treated like the customer-of-the-month. Fate dropped three of Southwest's most focused 'proposal-planner flight attendants' on me to help secure this wonderful second chance at true love. I would ask Shayna to marry me on a Southwest flight. Now all I had left to figure out was when.

Thanks to Southwest's finest, I had all the necessary guidelines to help ensure I could pull off the proposal without tipping Shayna off or disrupting the pilot's job.

We put together an entire skit that Jill and the other two attendants felt confident Southwest would be able to help me pull off, no matter when I flew or what crew was working the flight.

I should mention, if there's one thing Shayna dreads, it's being put on center stage, especially in public. Even the possibility of three or four people watching her open birthday gifts can fill her with nervous anxiety. However, I decided Shayna's dread of "being on display" and my humorous sarcasm would be the ultimate perfect recipe for a shocking true surprise event.

The Southwest ladies and I devised a plan where once the plane was in air, an attendant would start some fun with the passengers (as they often do), suggesting a game of 'Simon Says' to lighten spirits. Then they would ask for volunteers to start off the game and fake an attempt to select Shayna. However, keeping in mind there's absolutely no way she'd stand up in front of hundreds of complete strangers, I'd jump in and offer to take the spotlight off of her.

Then, making my way to the front of the aircraft, the attendant would ask that I briefly introduce myself and start directing a game of 'Simon Says,' secretly leading it into an unexpected marriage proposal.

Acting unsure of myself, I'd order: "Simon says…, put one hand in your pocket."

It was amazing almost every passenger followed my orders from a six-year-old girl in row five to a grandfather in row twenty two

"Simon says…, IF YOU HAVE A RING IN YOUR POCKET pull it out and hold it up."

The once agreeable audience now began to stare in bewilderment.

Then, the big moment: "Simon says, if you're madly in love with the woman sitting next to you, get on your knee and ask her to marry you!"

Of course if needed, I had one more command: *"Simon Says…, Shayna, say YES!"*

At 43 years old, my life up to that moment had already been quite a trip. And now, after embracing one of life's great surprise moments, I had officially bought a ticket for my next great flight of a lifetime.

Oh, and one more thing. She said Yes!

Then, I'll Know I Did My Job

"Kevin, I think about my dad every day."

While writing those stories of flying's highs and lows, an old memory came back to me of the very first flight I took after Pamela's funeral.

Minutes before 6 am on a Thursday morning, I rose up out of bed and floated down the stairs in a complete daze, my hair sticking up all over the place and my eyes practically glued shut. I just wanted to sneak downstairs before the roommates woke up, so I could feel in control of the rat race ahead. After the blood started flowing and a few Diet Cokes were roaring through my veins, I was in the routine of morning madness. One after another, each of my kids came shuffling into the kitchen. It only took minutes for multiple TVs to be playing and the onslaught of breakfast requests to be ringing in my ears, as I hustled back and forth between the pantry, the kitchen cabinets, and the breakfast table. When I opened the refrigerator to grab the morning supply of apple juice something caught my eye. It was an invite card behind a goofy magnet that stuck out among the many pieces of artwork from school projects the kids had taped up. Something about that moment made me finally take in that card. Above all the noise outside my head only one thing was echoing inside: *Oh my lord. Finally, a break!*

That card was a wedding invitation to my cousin Brendan's wedding back in Philadelphia. I don't know if I'd hung it up there, or maybe my mom had the last time she visited. But I am sure I'd walked by it for weeks, either ignoring it or thinking, *Yeah, right, can't wait to fly three kids to a wedding and spend the weekend chasing after them as family members ask me how we're all doing. What a fun time.* Something about this morning allowed me to register that this was not an invitation to another overwhelming day. *No, dummy, this is your chance, your big chance, for A BREAK.*

I called my parents later that day to talk to them about Brendon's wedding, a wedding I'd never miss any other time in my life. My parents, who are always the voice of reason (even when I'd rather not hear it), agreed this was a unique chance for me to take a break and just breathe for a few days. This would also be my first trip while leaving the kids behind since losing Pamela. The choice to go weighed heavily on my conscience, but I knew I needed a "time out," both mentally and physically. I also rationalized my decision with knowing how bad I'd feel if I didn't attend the wedding, since Brendan, as did everyone else in my immediate family, made sure to be by my side at Pamela's funeral. And lastly, I couldn't deny that the trip would be one heck of a good time, since all my aunts, uncles, and cousins that I closely grew up with would be there.

My mom put it very simply: "Kevin, you need to go. The family worries about you and it would mean a lot to everyone including Brendan to see you in person and know you're okay."

That's all I needed to hear. If I had any concern or guilt over leaving the kids, it was now washed away. Knowing I'd be giving back to my relatives, in a very tiny manner, the huge outpouring of love and support the kids and I had received during our time of need, made it easier to go. Plus, Brendan was one of the last of my cousins to get married, and the McAteers and O'Briens know how to party on a wedding day. *Woohoo, I'm getting a chance to breathe!*

A month later, there I was, entering this beautiful Catholic cathedral in downtown Philadelphia. Walking inside, I was completely mesmerized by its marble ceilings, so high they had to be touching heaven. For the first time in a long time, my life's 'play-back button' was pressed. Sitting in a pew with my Mom, Dad, and my brother Keith, I was surrounded by visions of childhood. Slowly, I shifted my eyes around the hundreds in church that day; Uncle Pat behind us to the right, cousin Timmy a few rows to the left, Aunt Sally in the front of the church gleaming with pride as her little boy Brendan was about to enter the holy sacrament of marriage. Sadly, missing from this close group of loved ones were my grandparents. Remembering them, I floated back to joyous memories of holidays spent being crammed together in a tiny Philadelphia row-home and, for a moment, I was the boy I'd been growing up. I was surrounded by those who molded me into the man I am today; the ones who taught me how to love, how to laugh, how to dream, and how to walk a straight line in life. As we sat waiting for the ceremony to start, my mind jumped from childhood memories to thoughts of my own children at home in Raleigh. I could feel my emotions rising and my heart rate increasing and within that instant, it felt as if Jesus was right there next to me, placing his hand on my shoulder and whispering in my ear, "*Take a break my son; let's slow down for today.*" Now surrounded by angels in God's house, just a dozen weeks from losing a part of my soul, I felt at peace.

As the ceremony went on, I did feel a bit off key, smiling at inopportune times, then wrestling a knot out of my throat as the realization hit that the owner of this Cathedral is the one Pamela now sits closest to. Deep into the ceremony my cousin Heather approached the microphone at the altar. "Let us pray for those in need and loved ones who have passed before us." I knew all eyes would be on me, both in caring support and in tearful sharing of my pain. My cousin continued, "Let us pray for Nanny and Pop Pop," my grandparents who'd passed some ten years earlier, the closest loved ones to me who now shared a room in heaven's house. I knew what was coming next, "Let us pray for Pamela McAteer and all those she loved and left behind." Sometimes you hide in a room of hundreds, other times you find this unexplainable strength when you feel the center of attention in such a big crowd. Mom's hand moved slightly over mine as we stood resting our hands on the back of the pew in front of us. I felt a slow leak from the corner of my eye, but different from the last time so many from my family gathered in a church. I was still in a good place, and I was going to slow down and take a break from grieving so intensely. I was okay.

I made it through the ceremony, and was able to soak in the great celebration and new life Brendan was embarking on. Now it was time to enjoy a typical McAteer wedding, surrounded by dancing, storytelling, and a whole lot of eating and drinking. I had taken my first breath, and was relaxed and laughing and living in the moment. I had finally let myself go and let my guard down. That's when grieving and responsibility hit me like a double-barreled shot in the chest.

At the beginning of the dinner service, one of the local priests, who was close to much of the family, got up to say a prayer. He prayed and commented on my Uncle Franie, Brendan's father, who passed away when Brendan, Michael, and Heather were very young. Michael was Brendan's best man and he was next to the microphone to give the toast. I felt a bit vulnerable, reminded that Uncle Franie's early passing had left my three cousins in a situation similar to the one life had placed on my three kids.

Michael's speech was a classic; stories of growing up that made the whole room laugh, and a few from the recent past that you could tell were well-kept secrets until now. There were also a couple you wondered where they were headed, and worried he was about to get Brendan into his first marital fight, before they even got to eat wedding cake. Michael ended his serious gesture of brotherly love, hilarious jokes, and crazy boyhood memories with this: "And Brendan, I know Dad is looking down on you right now, and he's so proud of you and the woman you've chosen to be your wife, to walk the rest of life with together!"

I sat there stunned; Uncle Franie had passed away about 25 years ago. I just glared at the floor in what was now a dimly-lit ballroom, music playing, and banquet servers walking through the room clanging dinner plates onto the tables. Through all the noise and conversations going on around me I was having the quietest one-on-one discussion with myself. I now knew how to judge my efforts as a single father, my responsibility as a widower with three young children. I now knew what it took to look at the reflection of that man, that father in the mirror and be able to say: *Pamela, I followed through on my promise, those final words to you as I kissed you goodbye, that I would see this through. I honored all the love you gave us.*

Parenting, the job we all say never ends. Parenting, the responsibility that often feels too mammoth for one person to handle. I could now live with an end in mind. No matter what Kevin Patrick, Amanda, or Christopher do for a living when they grow up, no matter what kind of grades are on their report cards, no matter how many strong relationships they build, or tough moments they experience from mistakes they make, it will be on that day I will know, *I did my job as their father.* That moment when I am sitting at a banquet table staring into a spotlight on stage, when one of them has made the commitment of a lifetime of love with another, surrounded by family and friends, and one of them turns with the microphone pressed to their lips and says: *I know Mommy is looking down and is proud of the person you've become, and I know she's smiling at who you have chosen to walk with by your side for the rest of your life."*

As the night went on, I never let the weight of grieving drown out the fun I was having with my family. The reception was coming to an end and I found my cousin Michael walking down the hallway alone, about to go back into the party. We gave each other a big hug, I said, "I have to thank you."

He interrupted me. "Man, we all loved Pamela and it was important to Brendan that we honor her during the mass."

"I appreciate your honoring Pamela, too. But I was thanking you for reminding me that even 20 years from now she'll still be a part of who Kevin, Amanda, and Christopher are, and she'll still get to share in their most special moments."

He turned, looked directly into my eyes, and said, "Kevin, I think about my dad every day."

Honey. You would be proud. I did good.

CPSIA information can be obtained at www.ICGtesting.com
Printed in the USA
LVOW11s2106210714

395200LV00004B/114/P